Contents

Curried cod

Prep: 10 mins **Cook:** 25 mins

Serves 4

Ingredients

- 1 tbsp oil
- 1 onion, chopped
- 2 tbsp medium curry powder
- thumb-sized piece ginger, peeled and finely grated
- 3 garlic cloves, crushed
- 2 x 400g cans chopped tomatoes
- 400g can chickpeas
- 4 cod fillets (about 125-150g each)
- zest 1 lemon, then cut into wedges
- handful coriander, roughly chopped

Method

STEP 1

Heat the oil in a large, lidded frying pan. Cook the onion over a high heat for a few mins, then stir in the curry powder, ginger and garlic. Cook for another 1-2 mins until fragrant, then stir in the tomatoes, chickpeas and some seasoning.

STEP 2

Cook for 8-10 mins until thickened slightly, then top with the cod. Cover and cook for another 5-10 mins until the fish is cooked through. Scatter over the lemon zest and coriander, then serve with the lemon wedges to squeeze over.

Lentil shepherd's pie with celeriac & butter bean mash

Prep: 15 mins **Cook:** 55 mins

Serves 4

Ingredients

For the lentils

- 100g red lentils
- 2 leeks , chopped
- 4 celery sticks, chopped
- 1 reduced-salt vegetable stock cube
- 150ml red wine
- 3 heaped tbsp tomato purée
- 1 tbsp chopped thyme

For the topping

- 800g celeriac , peeled and chopped (as for cooking potatoes)
- 210g can butter beans , drained
- 50g light cream cheese
- green veg, such as broccoli , to serve (optional)

Method

STEP 1

Boil the celeriac until tender when tested with the point of a knife, adding the beans for the final 5 mins of cooking. Drain and roughly mash with the cream cheese until the cheese is well mixed, but the veg is still a little chunky.

STEP 2

Meanwhile, tip the lentils into a pan with the leeks, celery and stock cube. Pour in the red wine and 600ml water, and add the tomato purée and thyme. Bring to the boil, cover the pan and simmer for 20-25 mins until the lentils are soft and pulpy. Towards the end of cooking, add a splash more water if they are drying out.

STEP 3

Heat oven to 200C/180C fan/gas 6. Spoon the lentils into the base of 4 individual pie dishes, then top with the celeriac mash, smoothing it to the edge of the dishes. Bake for 35 mins until bubbling and golden, then serve with a green veg such as broccoli, if you like.

Quinoa chilli with avocado & coriander

Prep:10 mins **Cook:**45 mins

Serves 2

Ingredients

- 1 tbsp rapeseed oil
- 1 large onion , sliced
- 2 large garlic cloves , chopped
- 1 green pepper , chopped
- ½-1 tsp smoked paprika
- ½-1 tsp chilli powder
- 2 tsp cumin
- 2 tsp coriander
- 400g can chopped tomatoes
- ½ tsp dried oregano
- 2 tsp vegetable bouillon powder (check the label if you're vegan)
- 80g quinoa , rinsed under cold water
- 400g can black beans , drained and rinsed
- generous handful of coriander , chopped
- 2 tbsp bio yogurt or coconut yogurt (optional)
- 1 small avocado , stoned, peeled and sliced

Method

STEP 1

Heat the oil in a non-stick frying pan and fry the onion and garlic for 8 mins. Add the pepper and spices to taste and fry for 1 min more.

STEP 2

Tip in the tomatoes and a can of water, stir in the oregano, bouillon and quinoa, bring to the boil, then cover and simmer for 20 mins.

STEP 3

Stir in the black beans and cook, uncovered, for 5 mins more. Add most of the coriander, then serve topped with the yogurt (if using), the remaining coriander and the avocado slices.

Meatball & tomato soup

Prep: 5 mins **Cook:** 15 mins

Serves 4

Ingredients

- 1½ tbsp rapeseed oil
- 1 onion, finely chopped
- 2 red peppers, deseeded and sliced
- 1 garlic clove, crushed
- ½ tsp chilli flakes
- 2 x 400g cans chopped tomatoes
- 100g giant couscous
- 500ml hot vegetable stock
- 12 pork meatballs
- 150g baby spinach
- ½ small bunch of basil
- grated parmesan, to serve (optional)

Method

STEP 1

Heat the oil in a saucepan. Fry the onion and peppers for 7 mins, then stir through the garlic and chilli flakes and cook for 1 min. Add the tomatoes, giant couscous and veg stock and bring to a simmer.

STEP 2

Season to taste, then add the meatballs and spinach. Simmer for 5-7 mins or until cooked through. Ladle into bowls and top with the basil and some parmesan, if you like.

Curried chicken pie

Prep: 20 mins **Cook:** 25 mins

Serves 4

Ingredients

- 2 tbsp cold pressed rapeseed oil
- 500g chicken breasts , cut into chunks
- 4 spring onions , sliced
- 3 garlic cloves , grated
- thumb-sized piece ginger , grated
- 1 tbsp curry powder
- 1 large head broccoli , cut into florets, top of stalk thinly sliced
- 1 tsp soy sauce
- 250ml low-fat coconut milk , plus a splash
- 250ml chicken stock
- 1 heaped tsp cornflour mixed with 1 tbsp hot water
- 4 large handfuls kale
- 4 sheets filo pastry
- ½ tbsp nigella seeds

Method

STEP 1

Heat oven to 220C/200C fan/gas 7. Pour 1 tbsp oil into a flameproof casserole dish. Add the chicken, season and fry for 4-5 mins on a medium heat, turning, until lightly browned. Remove with tongs and set aside.

STEP 2

Pour another ½ tbsp oil into the casserole dish and add the spring onions. Fry gently for a couple of mins, then stir in the garlic, ginger and curry powder. Cook for 1 min, then tip the chicken back into the pan, along with the broccoli, soy sauce, coconut milk, chicken stock and cornflour mixture. Bring to the boil, then stir in the kale. Once the kale has wilted, take the dish off the heat.

STEP 3

Mix the remaining oil with the splash of coconut milk. Unravel the pastry. Brush each sheet lightly with the oil mixture, then scrunch up and sit on top of the pie mixture. Scatter over the nigella seeds, then cook in the oven for 12 mins, or until the pastry is a deep golden brown. Leave to stand for a couple of mins before serving.

Vegan shepherd's pie

Prep: 30 mins **Cook:** 1 hr and 20 mins Cook time is 1 hr, 45 mins if making two large pies

Serves 8 (makes eight individual or two large pies)

Ingredients

- 1.2kg floury potatoes, such as Maris Piper or King Edward
- 50ml vegetable oil
- 30g dried porcini mushrooms, soaked in hot water for 15 mins, then drained (reserve the liquid)
- 2 large leeks, chopped
- 2 small onions, chopped
- 4 medium carrots (about 300g), cut into small cubes
- 1 vegetable stock cube (make sure it's vegan - we used Kallo)
- 3 garlic cloves, crushed
- 2 tbsp tomato purée
- 2 tsp smoked paprika
- 1 small butternut squash, peeled and cut into small cubes
- ½ small pack marjoram or oregano, leaves picked and roughly chopped
- ½ small pack thyme, leaves picked
- ½ small pack sage, leaves picked and roughly chopped
- 4 celery sticks, chopped
- 400g can chickpeas
- 300g frozen peas
- 300g frozen spinach
- 20ml olive oil
- small pack flat-leaf parsley, chopped
- tomato ketchup, to serve (optional)

Method

STEP 1

Put the unpeeled potatoes in a large saucepan, cover with water, bring to the boil and simmer for 40 mins until the skins start to split. Drain and leave to cool a little.

STEP 2

Meanwhile, heat the vegetable oil in a large heavy-based sauté pan or flameproof casserole dish. Add the mushrooms, leeks , onions, carrots and the stock cube and cook gently for 5 mins , stirring every so often. If it starts to stick, reduce the heat and stir more frequently, scraping the bits from the bottom. The veg should be soft but not mushy.

STEP 3

Add the garlic, tomato purée, paprika, squash and herbs. Stir and turn the heat up a bit, cook for 3 mins, add the celery, then stir and cook for a few more mins.

STEP 4

Tip in the chickpeas along with the water in the can and reserved mushroom stock. Add the peas and spinach and stir well. Cook for 5 mins, stirring occasionally, then season, turn off and set aside. There should still be plenty of liquid and the veg should be bright and a little firm.

STEP 5

Peel the potatoes and discard the skin. Mash 200g with a fork and stir into the veg. Break the rest of the potatoes into chunks, mix with the olive oil and parsley and season.

STEP 6

Divide the filling into the pie dishes and top with the potatotes. Heat oven to 190C/170C fan/gas 5 and bake the pies for 40-45 mins, until the top is golden and the filling is heated through. If making individual pies, check after 20 mins. Best served with tomato ketchup – as all great shepherd's pies are.

Crispy chilli turkey noodles

Prep:5 mins **Cook:**15 mins

Serves 4

Ingredients

- 2 tbsp sesame oil
- 500g turkey mince
- 5cm piece ginger, grated
- 1 large garlic clove, crushed
- 3 tbsp honey

- 3 tbsp soy sauce
- 1 tbsp hot sriracha chilli sauce
- 350g dried udon noodles
- 2 limes, juiced, plus wedges to serve (optional)
- 2 large carrots, peeled and cut into matchsticks
- 4 spring onions, shredded
- 1 small bunch coriander, sliced (optional)

Method

STEP 1

Heat 1 tbsp oil in a large non-stick frying pan over a high heat. Once hot, add the turkey mince to the pan and fry for 10-12 mins until golden brown and crispy, breaking up the meat with a wooden spoon as you go. Add the ginger and garlic to the pan and cook for 1 min. Stir in the honey, soy and chilli sauce and cook for 2 mins.

STEP 2

Meanwhile, bring a large pan of water to the boil, add the noodles and cook following pack instructions. Drain and toss the noodles with the remaining 1 tbsp oil and all the lime juice, then divide between bowls. Top with the crispy turkey mince, carrot, onion and coriander. Serve with extra lime wedges for squeezing over, if you like.

Orzo & tomato soup

Prep:5 mins **Cook:**25 mins

Serves 4

Ingredients

- 2 tbsp olive oil
- 1 onion, chopped
- 2 celery sticks, chopped
- 2 garlic cloves, crushed
- 1 tbsp tomato purée
- 400g can chopped tomatoes
- 400g can chickpeas
- 150g orzo pasta

- 700ml vegetable stock
- 2 tbsp basil pesto
- crusty bread, to serve

Method

STEP 1

Heat 1 tbsp olive oil in a large saucepan. Add the onion and celery and fry for 10-15 mins, or until starting to soften, then add the garlic and cook for 1 min more. Stir in all the other ingredients, except for the pesto and remaining oil, and bring to the boil.

STEP 2

Reduce the heat and leave to simmer for 6-8 mins, or until the orzo is tender. Season to taste, then ladle into bowls.

STEP 3

Stir the remaining oil with the pesto, then drizzle over the soup. Serve with chunks of crusty bread.

Chickpea soup with chunky gremolata

Prep:15 mins **Cook:**30 mins

Serves 4

Ingredients

- 2 tbsp cold-pressed rapeseed oil
- 3 onions , chopped (about 340g)
- 3 x 400g cans chickpeas , don't drain off the liquid
- 3 large cloves garlic , finely grated
- 1 red chilli , seeded and chopped
- 2 tsp ground coriander
- 1 tsp cumin seeds
- 4 tsp vegetable bouillon powder
- 1 aubergine , finely cubed (350g)
- 2 tbsp tahini
- 210g can chickpeas , drained

- 100g cherry tomatoes , cut into quarters
- 1 lemon , zested and half juiced
- 15g parsley , finely chopped
- 3 tbsp chopped mint leaves
- smoked paprika , for dusting

Method

STEP 1

Heat 1 tbsp oil in a large pan and fry the onions for 10 mins to soften. Tip the 3 cans of chickpeas into the pan and stir in 2 of the grated garlic cloves, the chilli, coriander and cumin along with the bouillon powder, aubergine and 1½ cans of water. Cover and simmer for 15-20 mins until the aubergine is tender, then remove from the heat, add the tahini and blitz with a hand blender until smooth.

STEP 2

Meanwhile, make the gremolata. Tip the small can of chickpeas into a bowl add the tomatoes, lemon zest and juice, parsley and mint with the remaining oil and garlic.

STEP 3

If you're following our Healthy Diet Plan, spoon half the soup into two bowls or large flasks and top with or pack up half the gremolata and a sprinkling of paprika. Cool and chill the remaining soup for another day on the plan. Reheat the soup in a pan or microwave to serve.

Pasta arrabbiata with aubergine

Prep:8 mins **Cook:**35 mins

Serves 2

Ingredients

- 1 tbsp cold-pressed rapeseed oil
- 1 large onion , finely chopped (160g)
- 2 large garlic cloves , finely grated
- 1 tsp chilli flakes
- 1 tsp smoked paprika
- 400g can chopped tomatoes

- 1 tsp vegetable bouillon powder
- 1 aubergine , chopped
- 150g wholemeal penne or fusilli
- large handful of basil , plus extra to serve
- 25g parmesan or vegetarian Italian-style hard cheese, finely grated

Method

STEP 1

Heat the oil in a large non-stick pan, add the onions, cover and cook for 5 mins. Remove the lid and cook for 5 mins more, stirring frequently until softened. Add the garlic, chilli flakes and paprika, stir briefly, then tip in the tomatoes and a can of water. Stir in the bouillon and aubergine, then bring to a simmer, cover and cook for 20 mins.

STEP 2

Cook the penne in a pan of boiling water for 12 mins until al dente. Drain, reserving 60ml of the cooking water. Add the cooked penne to the sauce, and toss well with the basil and a little of the reserved water, if needed. Spoon into two shallow bowls, and serve topped with the cheese and some extra basil, if you like.

Chipotle chicken & slaw

Prep:25 mins **Cook:**40 mins

Serves 4

Ingredients

- 1 tbsp rapeseed oil
- 2 tbsp chipotle paste
- 1½ tbsp honey
- 8 chicken drumsticks
- 1 lime , zested and juiced
- 1 small avocado , stoned
- 2 tbsp fat-free Greek yogurt
- 125g each red and white cabbage , both shredded
- 1 large carrot , cut into matchsticks
- 3 spring onions , sliced

- 4 corn on the cobs , steamed, to serve (optional)

Method

STEP 1

Heat the oven to 200C/180C fan/gas 6. Whisk the oil, chipotle paste and honey together in a large bowl. Add the chicken and toss to coat, then spread out on a non-stick baking tray. Roast for 30 mins, turning halfway through.

STEP 2

Put the lime zest and juice, avocado flesh, yogurt and a good pinch of salt into a blender and blitz until completely smooth. Put the sauce in a large bowl with the cabbage, carrot and spring onion and toss to combine.

STEP 3

Serve the drumsticks with the slaw and steamed corn, if you like.

Jerk cod & creamed corn

Prep:12 mins **Cook:**25 mins

Serves 2

Ingredients

- 2 thick cod fillets (about 120g each)
- 1 tbsp olive oil
- 2 tsp jerk seasoning
- bunch spring onions
- 326g can sweetcorn , drained
- 2 tbsp single cream
- 20g parmesan , finely grated
- ½-1 small red chilli , deseeded and finely chopped
- ½ small bunch coriander , finely chopped
- lime wedges, to serve (optional)

Method

STEP 1

Heat the oven to 200C/180C fan/gas 6. Put the cod on a baking sheet and rub with half the oil, the jerk seasoning and some salt and pepper. Cook for 12-15 mins until cooked through and flaking.

STEP 2

Meanwhile, heat a griddle pan or non-stick frying pan over a high heat. Rub the remaining oil over the whole spring onions. Add to the pan and cook for 8-10 mins or until charred and beginning to soften. Keep warm on a plate.

STEP 3

Put the corn in a saucepan with the cream and warm through for 2 mins. Using a stick blender, roughly blitz the corn to a semi-smooth consistency. Stir though the parmesan, chilli and half the coriander, then season to taste.

STEP 4

Serve the cod with the charred spring onions, creamed corn and lime wedges for squeezing over, and scatter over the remaining coriander.

Two-minute breakfast smoothie

Prep: 2 mins No cook

Serves 2

Ingredients

- 1 banana
- 1 tbsp porridge oats
- 80g soft fruit (whatever you have – strawberries, blueberries, and mango all work well)
- 150ml milk
- 1 tsp honey
- 1 tsp vanilla extract

Method

STEP 1

Put all the ingredients in a blender and whizz for 1 min until smooth.

STEP 2

Pour the banana oat smoothie into two glasses to serve.

Hearty lentil one pot

Prep: 10 mins **Cook:** 1 hr

Serves 4

Ingredients

- 40g dried porcini mushrooms , roughly chopped
- 200g dried brown lentils
- 1 ½ tbsp chopped rosemary
- 3 tbsp rapeseed oil
- 2 large onions , roughly chopped
- 150g chestnut baby button mushrooms
- 4 garlic cloves , finely grated
- 2 tbsp vegetable bouillon powder
- 2 large carrots (350g), cut into chunks
- 3 celery sticks (165g), chopped
- 500g potatoes , cut into chunks
- 200g cavolo nero , shredded

Method

STEP 1

Cover the mushrooms in boiling water and leave to soak for 10 mins. Boil the lentils in a pan with plenty of water for 10 mins. Drain and rinse, then tip into a pan with the dried mushrooms and soaking water (don't add the last bit of the liquid as it can contain some grit), rosemary and 2 litres water. Season, cover and simmer for 20 mins.

STEP 2

Meanwhile, heat the oil in a large pan and fry the onions for 5 mins. Stir in the fresh mushrooms and garlic and fry for 5 mins more. Stir in the lentil mixture and bouillon powder, then add the carrots, celery and potatoes. Cover and cook for 20 mins, stirring often, until the veg and lentils are tender, topping up the water level if needed.

STEP 3

Remove any tough stalks from the cavolo nero, then add to the pan and cover and cook for 5 mins more. If you're following our Healthy Diet Plan, serve half in bowls, then chill the rest to eat another day. Will keep in the fridge for two to three days. Reheat in a pan until hot.

Slow-cooker chicken casserole

Prep: 10 mins **Cook:** 4 hrs and 15 mins - 7 hrs and 15 mins

Serves 2 adults + 2 children

Ingredients

- knob of butter
- ½ tbsp rapeseed or olive oil
- 1 large onion, finely chopped
- 1 ½ tbsp flour
- 650g boneless, skinless chicken thigh fillets
- 3 garlic cloves, crushed
- 400g baby new potatoes, halved
- 2 sticks celery, diced
- 2 carrots, diced
- 250g mushrooms, quartered
- 15g dried porcini mushroom, soaked in 50ml boiling water
- 500ml stock made with 2 very low salt chicken stock cubes (we used Kallo)
- 2 tsp Dijon mustard, plus extra to serve
- 2 bay leaves

Method

STEP 1

Heat a knob of butter and ½ tbsp rapeseed or olive oil in a large frying pan, cook 1 finely chopped large onion for 8-10 mins until softened and starting to caramelise.

STEP 2

Meanwhile, put 1 ½ tbsp flour and a little salt and pepper in a bowl and toss 650g boneless, skinless chicken thigh fillets in it.

STEP 3

Add 3 crushed garlic cloves and the chicken to the pan and cook for 4-5 mins more until the chicken is starting to brown.

STEP 4

Transfer to your slow cooker, along with 400g halved baby new potatoes, 2 diced celery sticks, 2 diced carrots, 250g quartered mushrooms, 15g dried and soaked porcini mushrooms with the 50ml soaking liquid, 500ml chicken stock, 2 tsp Dijon mustard and 2 bay leaves.

STEP 5

Give it a good stir. Cook on Low for 7 hours or High for 4 hours.

STEP 6

Remove the bay leaves and serve with a little Dijon mustard on the side.

Carrot biryani

Prep:10 mins **Cook:**15 mins

Serves 4

Ingredients

- 2 tbsp olive oil
- 1 onion , sliced
- 1 green chilli , chopped (deseeded if you don't like it very hot)
- 1 garlic clove , peeled
- 1 tbsp garam marsala
- 1 tsp turmeric
- 3 carrots , grated
- 2 x 200g pouch brown basmati rice
- 150g frozen peas
- 50g roasted cashews
- coriander and yogurt, to serve

Method

STEP 1

Heat the oil in a large frying pan, tip in the onion with a big pinch of salt and fry until softened, around 5 mins, then add the chilli and crush in the garlic and cook for 1 min more. Stir in the spices with a splash of water and cook for a couple of mins before adding the carrots and stirring well to coat in all of the spices and flavours.

STEP 2

Tip in the rice, peas and cashews, then use the back of your spoon to break up any clumps of rice and combine with the rest of the ingredients, cover and cook over a high heat for 5 mins (it's nice if a bit of rice catches on the base to give a bit of texture to the dish). Scatter over the coriander with spoonfuls of yogurt, then serve straight from the pan.

Prosciutto, kale & butter bean stew

Prep:5 mins **Cook:**20 mins

Serves 4

Ingredients

- 80g pack prosciutto , torn into pieces
- 2 tbsp olive oil
- 1 fennel bulb , sliced
- 2 garlic clove , crushed
- 1 tsp chilli flakes
- 4 thyme sprigs
- 150ml white wine or chicken stock
- 2 x 400g cans butter beans
- 400g can cherry tomatoes
- 200g bag sliced kale

Method

STEP 1

Fry the prosciutto in a dry saucepan over a high heat until crisp, then remove half with a slotted spoon and set aside. Turn the heat down to low, pour in the oil and tip in the fennel with a pinch of salt. Cook for 5 mins until softened, then throw in the garlic, chilli flakes and thyme and cook for a further 2 mins, then pour in the wine or stock and bring to a simmer.

STEP 2

Tip both cans of butter beans into the stew, along with their liquid, then add the tomatoes, season well and bring everything to a simmer. Cook, undisturbed, for 5 mins, then stir through the kale. Once wilted, ladle the stew into bowls, removing the thyme sprigs and topping each portion with the remaining prosciutto.

Tomato & spinach kitchari

Prep:10 mins **Cook:**40 mins

Serves 4

Ingredients

- 130g basmati rice
- 200g split red lentils
- 3 tbsp olive oil
- 1 onion , finely sliced
- 1 thumb-sized piece ginger , finely grated
- 2 garlic cloves , crushed
- 2 tsp turmeric
- 2 tsp ground coriander
- 2 tsp cumin seeds
- 1-2 tsp medium chilli powder
- 1.2l vegetable stock
- 150g cherry tomatoes
- 200g spinach
- 1 red chilli , finely chopped
- chapatis , to serve (optional)

Method

STEP 1

Tip the rice and lentils into a sieve and rinse thoroughly under cold, running water. Set aside.

STEP 2

Heat 1 tbsp of the oil in a large saucepan or casserole. Add the onion along with a pinch of salt and fry over a medium-high heat for 10 mins or until golden. Stir through the ginger, garlic, turmeric, ground coriander, half the cumin seeds and the chilli powder and fry for 1 min. Add the rice and lentils to the pan and pour in the stock, bring to a simmer then cover, turn down and cook for 25 mins, stirring now and then, until the lentils have turned creamy. Add the tomatoes and spinach and cook for 5 mins.

STEP 3

Heat the remaining oil in a small frying pan and add the remaining cumin seeds, cooking for 1 min. Spoon the lentils into four bowls, drizzle over the cumin oil and top with the chilli. Serve with warm chapatis, if you like.

Artichoke & aubergine rice

Prep: 15 mins **Cook:** 50 mins

Serves 6

Ingredients

- 60ml olive oil
- 2 aubergines , cut into chunks
- 1 large onion , finely chopped
- 2 garlic cloves , crushed
- small pack parsley , leaves picked, stalks finely chopped
- 2 tsp smoked paprika
- 2 tsp turmeric
- 400g paella rice
- 1 ½l Kallo vegetable stock
- 2 x 175g packs chargrilled artichokes
- 2 lemons 1 juiced, 1 cut into wedges to serve

Method

STEP 1

Heat 2 tbsp of the oil in a large non-stick frying pan or paella pan. Fry the aubergines until nicely coloured on all sides (add another tbsp of oil if the aubergine begins catching too much), then remove and set aside. Add another tbsp of oil to the pan and lightly fry the onion for 2-3 mins or until softened. Add the garlic and parsley stalks, cook for a few mins more, then stir in the spices and rice until everything is well coated. Heat for 2 mins, add half the stock and cook, uncovered, over a medium heat for 20 mins, stirring occasionally to prevent it from sticking.

STEP 2

Nestle the aubergine and artichokes into the mixture, pour over the rest of the stock and cook for 20 mins more or until the rice is cooked through. Chop the parsley leaves, stir through with the lemon juice and season well. Bring the whole pan to the table and spoon into bowls, with the lemon wedges on the side.

Healthy pancakes

Prep:15 mins **Cook:**30 mins

Makes 10-12

Ingredients

- 50g self-raising flour
- 50g wholemeal or wholegrain flour
- 2 small eggs, separated
- 150ml skimmed milk
- berries and low-fat yogurt or fromage frais to serve

Method

STEP 1

Sift the flours into a bowl or wide jug and tip any bits in the sieve back into the bowl. Add the egg yolks and a splash of milk then stir to a thick paste. Add the remaining milk a little at a time so you don't make lumps in the batter.

STEP 2

Whisk the egg whites until they stand up in stiff peaks, then fold them carefully into the batter – try not to squash out all the air.

STEP 3

Heat a non-stick pan over a medium heat and pour in enough batter to make a pancake about 10 cm across. Cook for just under a minute until bubbles begin to pop on the surface and the edges are looking a little dry. Carefully turn the pancake over. If it is a bit wet on top, it may squirt out a little batter as you do so. In that case, leave it on the other side a little longer. Keep warm while you make the remaining pancakes. Serve with your favourite healthy toppings.

Veggie yaki udon

Prep: 10 mins **Cook:** 15 mins

Serves 2

Ingredients

- 1½ tbsp sesame oil
- 1 red onion , cut into thin wedges
- 160g mangetout
- 70g baby corn , halved
- 2 baby pak choi , quartered
- 3 spring onions , sliced
- 1 large garlic clove , crushed
- ½ tbsp mild curry powder
- 4 tsp low-salt soy sauce
- 300g ready-to-cook udon noodles
- 1 tbsp pickled sushi ginger , chopped, plus 2 tbsp of the brine

Method

STEP 1

Heat the oil in a non-stick frying pan or wok over a high heat. Add the onion and fry for 5 mins. Stir in the mangetout, corn, pak choi and spring onions and cook for 5 mins more. Add the garlic, curry powder and soy sauce, and cook for another minute.

STEP 2

Add the udon noodles along with the ginger and reserved brine, and stir in 2-3 tbsp hot water until the noodles are heated through. Divide between bowls and serve.

Bombay potato frittata

Prep: 15 mins **Cook:** 35 mins

Serves 2

Ingredients

- 4 new potatoes , sliced into 5mm rounds
- 100g baby spinach , chopped
- 1 tbsp rapeseed oil
- 1 onion , halved and sliced
- 1 large garlic clove , finely grated
- ½ tsp ground coriander
- ½ tsp ground cumin
- ¼ tsp black mustard seeds
- ¼ tsp turmeric
- 3 tomatoes , roughly chopped
- 2 large eggs
- ½ green chilli , deseeded and finely chopped
- 1 small bunch of coriander , finely chopped
- 1 tbsp mango chutney
- 3 tbsp fat-free Greek yogurt

Method

STEP 1

Cook the potatoes in a pan of boiling water for 6 mins, or until tender. Drain and leave to steam-dry. Meanwhile, put the spinach in a heatproof bowl with 1 tbsp water. Cover and microwave for 3 mins on high, or until wilted.

STEP 2

Heat the rapeseed oil in a medium non-stick frying pan. Add the onion and cook over a medium heat for 10 mins until golden and sticky. Stir in the garlic, ground coriander, ground cumin, mustard seeds and turmeric, and cook for 1 min more. Add the tomatoes and wilted spinach and cook for another 3 mins, then add the potatoes.

STEP 3

Heat the grill to medium. Lightly beat the eggs with the chilli and most of the fresh coriander and pour over the potato mixture. Grill for 4-5 mins, or until golden and just set, with a very slight wobble in the middle.

STEP 4

Leave to cool, then slice into wedges. Mix the mango chutney, yogurt and remaining fresh coriander together. Serve with the frittata wedges.

Easy slow cooker chicken casserole

Prep: 10 mins **Cook:** 4 hrs - 8 hrs

Serves 4

Ingredients

- 1 leek, roughly chopped
- 1 carrot, roughly chopped
- 1 onion, roughly chopped
- 350g new potatoes, roughly chopped
- 6 skinless, boneless chicken thighs, chopped
- 500ml chicken stock
- 4 tbsp vegetable gravy granules

Method

STEP 1

Put the veg and chicken in a slow cooker. Pour the stock over and around the chicken thighs, then mix in the gravy granules to thicken it up (the sauce will be quite thick – use less gravy if you prefer a runnier casserole).

STEP 2

Switch the slow cooker to low and leave to cook for at least 4 hrs, or up to 8 hrs – try putting it on before you go to work, so that it's ready when you get home. Season well, then serve.

Slow-cooker vegetable lasagne

Prep: 30 mins **Cook:** 2 hrs and 30 mins - 3 hrs

Serves 4

Ingredients

- 1 tbsp rapeseed oil
- 2 onions, sliced
- 2 large garlic cloves, chopped
- 2 large courgettes, diced (400g)
- 1 red and 1 yellow pepper, deseeded and roughly sliced
- 400g can chopped tomatoes
- 2 tbsp tomato purée
- 2 tsp vegetable bouillon
- 15g fresh basil, chopped plus a few leaves
- 1 large aubergine, sliced across length or width for maximum surface area
- 6 wholewheat lasagne sheets (105g)
- 125g vegetarian buffalo mozzarella, chopped

Method

STEP 1

Heat 1 tbsp rapeseed oil in a large non-stick pan and fry 2 sliced onions and 2 chopped large garlic cloves for 5 mins, stirring frequently until softened.

STEP 2

Tip in 2 diced large courgettes, 1 red and 1 yellow pepper, both roughly sliced, and 400g chopped tomatoes with 2 tbsp tomato purée, 2 tsp vegetable bouillon and 15g chopped basil.

STEP 3

Stir well, cover and cook for 5 mins. Don't be tempted to add more liquid as plenty of moisture will come from the vegetables once they start cooking.

STEP 4

Slice 1 large aubergine. Lay half the slices of aubergine in the base of the slow cooker and top with 3 sheets of lasagne.

STEP 5

Add a third of the ratatouille mixture, then the remaining aubergine slices, 3 more lasagne sheets, then the remaining ratatouille mixture.

STEP 6

Cover and cook on High for 2½ - 3 hours until the pasta and vegetables are tender. Turn off the machine.

STEP 7

Scatter 125g vegetarian buffalo mozzarella over the vegetables then cover and leave for 10 mins to settle and melt the cheese.

STEP 8

Scatter with extra basil and serve with a handful of rocket.

Spiced halloumi & pineapple burger with zingy slaw

Prep:20 mins **Cook:**5 mins

Serves 2

Ingredients

- ½ red cabbage, grated
- 2 carrots, grated
- 100g radishes, sliced
- 1 small pack coriander, chopped
- 2 limes, juiced
- 1 tbsp cold-pressed rapeseed oil
- big pinch of chilli flakes
- 1 tbsp chipotle paste
- 60g halloumi, cut into 4 slices
- 2 small slices of fresh pineapple
- 1 Little Gem lettuce, divided into 4 lettuce cups, or 2 small seeded burger buns, cut in half, to serve (optional)

Method

STEP 1

Heat the barbecue. Put the cabbage, carrot, radish and coriander in a bowl. Pour over the lime juice, add ½ tbsp oil and the chilli flakes, then season with salt and pepper. Give everything a good mix with your hands. This can be done a few hours before and kept in the fridge.

STEP 2

Mix the remaining oil with the chipotle paste then coat the halloumi slices in the mixture. Put the halloumi slices on a sheet of foil and put on the barbecue with the pineapple (or use a searing hot griddle pan if cooking inside). Cook for 2 mins on each side until the cheese is golden, and the pineapple is beginning to caramelise. Brush the buns with the remaining chipotle oil, then put your burger buns, if using, cut-side down, on the barbecue for the last 30 seconds of cooking to toast.

STEP 3

Assemble your burgers with the lettuce or buns. Start with a handful of the slaw, then add halloumi and pineapple. Serve with the remaining slaw.

Low sugar chocolate sandwich cake

Prep:35 mins **Cook:**25 mins - 30 mins

Cuts into 12

Ingredients

For the cake

- 150ml rapeseed oil , plus extra for greasing
- 250g cooked beetroot
- 50g cocoa
- 140g plain wholewheat flour
- 100g plain white flour
- 50g ground almonds
- 200g xylitol , such as Total Sweet
- 2 tsp baking powder
- 1 tsp bicarbonate of soda
- 2 large eggs
- 2 tsp vanilla extract
- 50ml skimmed milk

For the chocolate cream

- 150ml pot natural bio-yogurt
- 2 tbsp cocoa
- 100g xylitol such as Total Sweet
- 150ml pot double cream

Method

STEP 1

Heat oven to 160C/140C/gas 3 and grease then line the base of two x 20cm sandwich tins with baking parchment. To start making the chocolate cream stir the yogurt with the cocoa and xylitol until completely blended then set aside while you make the cake. This helps to dissolve the xylitol granules.

STEP 2

To make the cake, first blitz the beetroot in a food processor until it resembles a thick puree. Tip in the cocoa, flours, ground almonds, xylitol, baking powder and soda and pulse briefly to mix the ingredients together.

STEP 3

Now add the eggs, the 150ml rapeseed oil, vanilla extract and milk, and blitz again to make a smooth liquid batter.

STEP 4

Divide the mixture evenly between the tins working quickly, as the baking powder activates once in contact with the liquid ingredients, then bake for 25-30 mins until a skewer poked into the middle of the cake comes out clean. Cool for few mins then remove from the tins and finish cooling on a wire rack. Once cold, carefully strip off the lining paper.

STEP 5

To finish the chocolate cream, whip the double cream until it holds its shape. Stir the cocoa mixture then fold in all but 2 tsp. Spread a third on top of one of the cold sponge cakes, top with the remaining sponge and spread with the rest of the chocolate cream to create a swirly finish. Dot over the reserved cocoa mixture and gently feather in with the end of a teaspoon. The cake will keep in the fridge for a couple of days, but return to room temperature before eating for the best taste and texture.

Super-quick sesame ramen

Prep:5 mins **Cook:**10 mins

Serves 1

Ingredients

- 80g pack instant noodles (look for an Asian brand with a flavour like sesame)
- 2 spring onions , finely chopped
- ½ head pak choi
- 1 egg
- 1 tsp sesame seeds
- chilli sauce , to serve

Method

STEP 1

Cook the noodles with the sachet of flavouring provided (or use stock instead of the sachet, if you have it). Add the spring onions and pak choi for the final min.

STEP 2

Meanwhile, simmer the egg for 6 mins from boiling, run it under cold water to stop it cooking, then peel it. Toast the sesame seeds in a frying pan.

STEP 3

Tip the noodles and greens into a deep bowl, halve the boiled egg and place on top. Sprinkle with sesame seeds, then drizzle with the sauce or sesame oil provided with the noodles, and chilli sauce, if using.

Smoky spiced veggie rice

Prep:15 mins **Cook:**1 hr

Serves 6

Ingredients

- 25g cashews

- 4 tbsp olive oil
- 1 corn cob
- 250g rainbow baby carrots , halved lengthways
- 2 red onions , finely chopped
- 2 celery sticks , finely chopped
- 2 large red peppers , finely sliced
- 3 garlic cloves , crushed
- 2 tbsp Cajun seasoning
- 1½ tbsp smoked paprika
- 1 tsp chipotle paste
- 2 tbsp tomato purée
- 200g heirloom cherry tomatoes , halved
- 400g can kidney beans , drained and rinsed
- 400g can cherry tomatoes
- 300g long-grain rice , washed
- 400ml vegetable or vegan stock
- 1 tbsp red wine vinegar (vegan varieties are readily available)
- 2 tbsp caster sugar
- 2 spring onions , finely sliced

Method

STEP 1

Dry-fry the cashews in a large saucepan or casserole dish over a medium heat until golden brown. Remove from the heat, leave to cool, then roughly chop. Heat 1 tbsp oil in the same pan over a high heat, then fry the corn on each side for 20 seconds to char. Remove from the pan, set aside, then tip in the carrots and fry for 5 mins. Remove from the pan and set aside.

STEP 2

Heat the rest of the oil in the same pan over a medium heat and fry the onions and celery for 10 mins until soft and slightly coloured. Tip in the peppers and garlic, then fry for another 5 mins before adding the Cajun seasoning, smoked paprika, chipotle paste and tomato purée. Fry for 1 min until the spices are fragrant, then add the cherry tomatoes and fry for another 2 mins.

STEP 3

Stir in the kidney beans, canned tomatoes, rice, stock, vinegar and sugar, then stir until everything is combined. Bring to the boil, then cover with a lid and simmer with a lid on for 35-40 mins on a medium-low heat, stirring halfway through, until the rice is cooked and liquid absorbed.

STEP 4

Slice the corn off the cob and mix it through the rice along with the carrots. Season and garnish with the spring onions and cashews.

Spiced chicken, spinach & sweet potato stew

Prep:15 mins **Cook:**40 mins

Serves 4

Ingredients

- 3 sweet potatoes, cut into chunks
- 190g bag spinach
- 1 tbsp sunflower oil
- 8 chicken thighs, skinless and boneless
- 500ml chicken stock

For the spice paste

- 2 onions, chopped
- 1 red chilli, chopped
- 1 tsp paprika
- thumb-sized piece ginger, grated
- 400g can tomatoes
- 2 preserved lemons, deseeded and chopped

To serve

- pumpkin seeds, toasted
- 2-3 preserved lemons, deseeded and chopped
- 4 naan bread, warmed

Method

STEP 1

Put the sweet potato in a large, deep saucepan over a high heat. Cover with boiling water and boil for 10 mins. Meanwhile, put all the paste ingredients in a food processor and blend until very finely chopped. Set aside until needed.

STEP 2

Put the spinach in a large colander in the sink and pour the sweet potatoes and their cooking water over it to drain the potatoes and wilt the spinach at the same time. Leave to steam-dry.

STEP 3

Return the saucepan to the heat (no need to wash it first), then add the oil, followed by the spice paste. Fry the paste for about 5 mins until thickened, then add the chicken. Fry for 8-10 mins until the chicken starts to colour. Pour over the stock, bring to the boil and leave to simmer for 10 mins, stirring occasionally.

STEP 4

Check the chicken is cooked by cutting into one of the thighs and making sure it's white throughout with no signs of pink. Season with black pepper, then add the sweet potato. Leave to simmer for a further 5 mins. Meanwhile, roughly chop the spinach and add to the stew. At this point you can leave the stew to cool and freeze for up to 3 months, if you like.

STEP 5

Scatter over the pumpkin seeds and preserved lemons, and serve with warm naan bread on the side.

Prawn jambalaya

Prep:10 mins **Cook:**35 mins

Serves 2

Ingredients

- 1 tbsp rapeseed oil
- 1 onion , chopped
- 3 celery sticks , sliced
- 100g wholegrain basmati rice

- 1 tsp mild chilli powder
- 1 tbsp ground coriander
- ½ tsp fennel seeds
- 400g can chopped tomatoes
- 1 tsp vegetable bouillon powder
- 1 yellow pepper , roughly chopped
- 2 garlic cloves , chopped
- 1 tbsp fresh thyme leaves
- 150g pack small prawns , thawed if frozen
- 3 tbsp chopped parsley

Method

STEP 1

Heat the oil in a large, deep frying pan. Add the onion and celery, and fry for 5 mins to soften. Add the rice and spices, and pour in the tomatoes with just under 1 can of water. Stir in the bouillon powder, pepper, garlic and thyme.

STEP 2

Cover the pan with a lid and simmer for 30 mins until the rice is tender and almost all the liquid has been absorbed. Stir in the prawns and parsley, cook briefly to heat through, then serve.

Mediterranean turkey-stuffed peppers

Prep:20 mins **Cook:**30 mins

Serves 2

Ingredients

- 2 red peppers (about 220g)
- 1 ½ tbsp olive oil, plus an extra drizzle
- 240g lean turkey breast mince (under 8% fat)
- ½ small onion, chopped
- 1 garlic clove, grated
- 1 tsp ground cumin
- 3-4 mushrooms, sliced

- 400g can chopped tomatoes
- 1 tbsp tomato purée
- 1 chicken stock cube
- handful fresh oregano leaves
- 60g mozzarella, grated
- 150g green vegetables (spinach, kale, broccoli, mangetout or green beans), to serve

Method

STEP 1

Heat oven to 190C/170C fan/gas 5. Halve the peppers lengthways, then remove the seeds and core but keep the stalks on. Rub the peppers with a drizzle of olive oil and season well. Put on a baking tray and roast for 15 mins.

STEP 2

Meanwhile, heat 1 tbsp olive oil in a large pan over a medium heat. Fry the mince for 2-3 mins, stirring to break up the chunks, then tip onto a plate.

STEP 3

Wipe out your pan, then heat the rest of the oil over a medium-high heat. Add the onion and garlic, stir-fry for 2-3 mins, then add the cumin and mushrooms and cook for 2-3 mins more.

STEP 4

Tip the mince back into the pan and add the chopped tomatoes and tomato purée. Crumble in the stock cube and cook for 3-4 mins, then add the oregano and season. Remove the peppers from the oven and fill them with as much of the mince as you can. (Don't worry if some spills out it – it will go satisfyingly crisp in the oven.) Top with the cheese and return to the oven for 10-15 mins until the cheese starts to turn golden.

STEP 5

Carefully slide the peppers onto a plate and serve alongside a pile of your favourite greens blanched, boiled or steamed.

Mango sorbet

Prep:15 mins plus freezing

Serves 8

Ingredients

- 3 large, ripe mangoes
- 200g caster sugar
- 1 lime , juiced

Method

STEP 1

Peel the mangoes with a vegetable peeler, cut as much of the flesh away from the stone as you can, put it in a food processor or blender.

STEP 2

Add the sugar, lime juice and 200ml water. Blend for a few minutes, until the mango is very smooth and the sugar has dissolved – rub a little of the mixture between your fingers, if it still feels gritty, blend for a little longer. Pour into a container and put in the freezer for a few hours.

STEP 3

Scrape the sorbet back into the blender (if it's very solid, leave at room temperature for 5-10 mins first). Whizz until you have a slushy mixture, then pour back into the tin and freeze for another hour or so.

STEP 4

Repeat step 3. Freeze until solid (another hour or two). Will keep covered in the freezer for three months.

Creamy chicken & asparagus braise

Prep:10 mins **Cook:**20 mins - 25 mins

Serves 2

Ingredients

- 1 tbsp rapeseed oil
- 2 skinless chicken breasts (about 150g each)
- 10 medium asparagus spears , each cut into 3

- 1 large or 2 small leeks , well washed and thickly sliced
- 3 celery sticks , sliced
- 200ml reduced-salt vegetable bouillon
- 140g frozen peas
- 1 egg yolk
- 4 tbsp natural bio yogurt
- 1 garlic clove , finely grated
- ⅓ small pack fresh tarragon , chopped
- new potatoes , to serve (optional)

Method

STEP 1

Heat the oil in a large non-stick frying pan and fry the chicken for 5 mins, turning to brown both sides.

STEP 2

Add the asparagus (reserve the tips), leeks and celery, pour in the bouillon and simmer for 10 mins. Add the asparagus tips and peas, and cook for 5 mins more.

STEP 3

Meanwhile, stir the egg yolk with the yogurt and garlic. Stir the yogurt mixture into the vegetables and add the tarragon. Divide between two warm plates, then place the chicken on top of the vegetables. Serve with new potatoes, if you like.

Low-fat chicken biryani

Prep:25 mins **Cook:**1 hr and 35 mins Plus marinating

Serves 5

Ingredients

- 3 garlic cloves , finely grated
- 2 tsp finely grated ginger
- ¼ tsp ground cinnamon
- 1 tsp turmeric
- 5 tbsp natural yogurt

- 600g boneless, skinless chicken breast , cut into 4-5cm pieces
- 2 tbsp semi-skimmed milk
- good pinch saffron
- 4 medium onions
- 4 tbsp rapeseed oil
- ½ tsp hot chilli powder
- 1 cinnamon stick , broken in half
- 5 green cardamom pods , lightly bashed to split
- 3 cloves
- 1 tsp cumin seed
- 280g basmati rice
- 700ml chicken stock
- 1 tsp garam masala
- handful chopped coriander leaves

Method

STEP 1

In a mixing bowl, stir together the garlic, ginger, cinnamon, turmeric and yogurt with some pepper and ¼ tsp salt. Tip in the chicken pieces and stir to coat (see step 1, above). Cover and marinate in the fridge for about 1 hr or longer if you have time. Warm the milk to tepid, stir in the saffron and set aside.

STEP 2

Heat oven to 200C/180C fan/gas 6. Slice each onion in half lengthways, reserve half and cut the other half into thin slices. Pour 1½ tbsp of the oil onto a baking tray, scatter over the sliced onion, toss to coat, then spread out in a thin, even layer (step 2). Roast for 40-45 mins, stirring halfway, until golden.

STEP 3

When the chicken has marinated, thinly slice the reserved onion. Heat 1 tbsp oil in a large sauté or frying pan. Fry the onion for 4-5 mins until golden. Stir in the chicken, a spoonful at a time, frying until it is no longer opaque, before adding the next spoonful (this helps to prevent the yogurt from curdling). Once the last of the chicken has been added, stir-fry for a further 5 mins until everything looks juicy. Scrape any sticky bits off the bottom of the pan, stir in the chilli powder, then pour in 100ml water, cover and simmer on a low heat for 15 mins. Remove and set aside.

STEP 4

Cook the rice while the chicken simmers. Heat another 1 tbsp oil in a large sauté pan, then drop in the cinnamon stick, cardamom, cloves and cumin seeds. Fry briefly until their aroma is released. Tip in the rice (step 3) and fry for 1 min, stirring constantly. Stir in the stock and bring to the boil. Lower the heat and simmer, covered, for about 8 mins or until all the stock has been absorbed. Remove from the heat and leave with the lid on for a few mins, so the rice can fluff up. Stir the garam masala into the remaining 1½ tsp oil and set aside. When the onions are roasted, remove and reduce oven to 180C/160C fan/gas 4.

STEP 5

Spoon half the chicken and its juices into an ovenproof dish, about 25 x 18 x 6cm, then scatter over a third of the roasted onions. Remove the whole spices from the rice, then layer half of the rice over the chicken and onions. Drizzle over the spiced oil. Spoon over the rest of the chicken and a third more onions. Top with the remaining rice (step 4) and drizzle over the saffron-infused milk. Scatter over the rest of the onions, cover tightly with foil and heat through in the oven for about 25 mins. Serve scattered with the mint and coriander.

Slow cooker shepherd's pie

Prep:1 hr **Cook:**5 hrs

Serves 4

Ingredients

- 1 tbsp olive oil
- 1 onion, finely chopped
- 3-4 thyme sprigs
- 2 carrots, finely diced
- 250g lean (10%) mince lamb or beef
- 1 tbsp plain flour
- 1 tbsp tomato purée
- 400g can lentils, or white beans
- 1 tsp Worcestershire sauce

For the topping

- 650g potatoes, peeled and cut into chunks
- 250g sweet potatoes, peeled and cut into chunks
- 2 tbsp half-fat crème fraîche

Method

STEP 1

Heat the slow cooker if necessary. Heat the oil in a large frying pan. Tip the onions and thyme sprigs and fry for 2-3 mins. Then add the carrots and fry together, stirring occasionally until the vegetables start to brown. Stir in the mince and fry for 1-2 mins until no longer pink. Stir in the flour then cook for another 1-2 mins. Stir in the tomato purée and lentils and season with pepper and the Worcestershire sauce, adding a splash of water if you think the mixture is too dry. Scrape everything into the slow cooker.

STEP 2

Meanwhile cook both lots of potatoes in simmering water for 12-13 minutes or until they are cooked through. Drain well and then mash with the crème fraîche. Spoon this on top of the mince mixture and cook on Low for 5 hours - the mixture should be bubbling at the sides when it is ready. Crisp up the potato topping under the grill if you like.

Chunky vegetable & brown rice soup

Prep: 18 mins **Cook:** 50 mins

Serves 4

Ingredients

- 2 tbsp cold-pressed rapeseed oil
- 1 medium onion , halved and sliced
- 2 garlic cloves , finely sliced
- 2 celery sticks , trimmed and thinly sliced
- 2medium carrots , cut into chunks
- 2 medium parsnips , cut into chunks
- 1 tbsp finely chopped thyme leaves
- 100g wholegrain rice

- 2medium leeks , sliced
- ½ small pack parsley , to garnish

Method

STEP 1

Heat the oil in a large non-stick pan and add the onion, garlic, celery, carrots, parsnips and thyme. Cover with a lid and cook gently for 15 mins, stirring occasionally, until the onions are softened and beginning to colour. Add the rice and pour in 1.2 litres cold water. Bring to the boil, then reduce the heat to a simmer and cook, uncovered, for 15 mins, stirring occasionally.

STEP 2

Season the soup with plenty of ground black pepper and salt to taste, then stir in the leeks. Return to a gentle simmer and cook for a further 5 mins or until the leeks have softened. Adjust the seasoning to taste and blitz half the soup with a stick blender, leaving the other half chunky, if you like. Top with the parsley and serve in deep bowls.

Curried spinach, eggs & chickpeas

Prep:15 mins **Cook:**35 mins

Serves 2

Ingredients

- 1 tbsp rapeseed oil
- 1 onion , thinly sliced
- 1 garlic clove , crushed
- 3cm piece ginger , peeled and grated
- 1 tsp ground turmeric
- 1 tsp ground coriander
- 1 tsp garam masala
- 1 tbsp ground cumin
- 450g tomatoes , chopped
- 400g can chickpeas , drained
- 1 tsp sugar
- 200g spinach
- 2 large eggs

- 3 tbsp natural yogurt
- 1 red chilli , finely sliced
- ½ small bunch of coriander , torn

Method

STEP 1

Heat the oil in a large frying pan or flameproof casserole pot over a medium heat, and fry the onion for 10 mins until golden and sticky. Add the garlic, ginger, turmeric, ground coriander, garam masala, cumin and tomatoes, and fry for 2 mins more. Add the chickpeas, 100ml water and the sugar and bring to a simmer. Stir in the spinach, then cover and cook for 20-25 mins. Season to taste.

STEP 2

Cook the eggs in a pan of boiling water for 7 mins, then rinse under cold running water to cool. Drain, peel and halve. Swirl the yogurt into the curry, then top with the eggs, chilli and coriander. Season.

Cabbage soup

Prep:20 mins **Cook:**50 mins

Serves 6

Ingredients

- 2 tbsp olive oil
- 1 large onion , finely chopped
- 2 celery sticks , finely chopped
- 1 large carrot , finely chopped
- 70g smoked pancetta , diced (optional)
- 1 large Savoy cabbage , shredded
- 2 fat garlic cloves , crushed
- 1 heaped tsp sweet smoked paprika
- 1 tbsp finely chopped rosemary
- 1 x 400g can chopped tomatoes
- 1.7l hot vegetable stock
- 1 x 400g can chickpeas , drained and rinsed

- shaved parmesan (or vegetarian alternative), to serve (optional)
- crusty bread , to serve (optional)

Method

STEP 1

Heat the oil in a casserole pot over a low heat. Add the onion, celery and carrot, along with a generous pinch of salt, and fry gently for 15 mins, or until the veg begins to soften. If you're using pancetta, add it to the pan, turn up the heat and fry for a few mins more until turning golden brown. Tip in the cabbage and fry for 5 mins, then stir through the garlic, paprika and rosemary and cook for 1 min more.

STEP 2

Tip the chopped tomatoes and stock into the pan. Bring to a simmer, then cook, uncovered, for 30 mins, adding the chickpeas for the final 10 mins. Season generously with salt and black pepper.

STEP 3

Ladle the soup into six deep bowls. Serve with the shaved parmesan and crusty bread, if you like.

Red pepper, squash & harissa soup

Prep: 15 mins **Cook:** 1 hr

Serves 6

Ingredients

- 1 small butternut squash (about 600-700g), peeled and cut into chunks
- 2 red pepper , roughly chopped
- 2 red onion , roughly chopped
- 3 tbsp rapeseed oil
- 3 garlic cloves in their skins
- 1 tbsp ground coriander
- 2 tsp ground cumin
- 1.2l chicken or vegetable stock
- 2 tbsp harissa paste

- 50ml double cream

Method

STEP 1

Heat oven to 180C/160C fan/gas 4. Put all the veg on a large baking tray and toss together with rapeseed oil, garlic cloves in their skins, ground coriander, ground cumin and some seasoning. Roast for 45 mins, moving the veg around in the tray after 30 mins, until soft and starting to caramelise. Squeeze the garlic cloves out of their skins. Tip everything into a large pan. Add the chicken or vegetable stock, harissa paste and double cream. Bring to a simmer and bubble for a few mins. Blitz the soup in a blender, check the seasoning and add more liquid if you need to. Serve swirled with extra cream and harissa.

Linguine with avocado, tomato & lime

Prep: 20 mins **Cook:** 10 mins

Serves 2

Ingredients

- 115g wholemeal linguine
- 1 lime, zested and juiced
- 1 avocado, stoned, peeled, and chopped
- 2 large ripe tomatoes, chopped
- ½ pack fresh coriander, chopped
- 1 red onion, finely chopped
- 1 red chilli, deseeded and finely chopped (optional)

Method

STEP 1

Cook the pasta according to pack instructions – about 10 mins. Meanwhile, put the lime juice and zest in a medium bowl with the avocado, tomatoes, coriander, onion and chilli, if using, and mix well.

STEP 2

Drain the pasta, toss into the bowl and mix well. Serve straight away while still warm, or cold.

Roasted roots & sage soup

Prep: 15 mins **Cook:** 45 mins

Serves 2

Ingredients

- 1 parsnip , peeled and chopped
- 2 carrots , peeled and chopped
- 300g turnip , swede or celeriac, chopped
- 4 garlic cloves , skin left on
- 1 tbsp rapeseed oil , plus ½ tsp
- 1 tsp maple syrup
- ¼ small bunch of sage , leaves picked, 4 whole, the rest finely chopped
- 750ml vegetable stock
- grating of nutmeg
- 1½ tbsp fat-free yogurt

Method

STEP 1

Heat the oven to 200C/180C fan/gas 6. Toss the root vegetables and garlic with 1 tbsp oil and season. Tip onto a baking tray and roast for 30 mins until tender. Toss with the maple syrup and the chopped sage, then roast for another 10 mins until golden and glazed. Brush the whole sage leaves with ½ tsp oil and add to the baking tray in the last 3-4 mins to crisp up, then remove and set aside.

STEP 2

Scrape the vegetables into a pan, squeeze the garlic out of the skins, discarding the papery shells, and add with the stock, then blend with a stick blender until very smooth and creamy. Bring to a simmer and season with salt, pepper and nutmeg.

STEP 3

Divide between bowls. Serve with a swirl of yogurt and the crispy sage leaves.

Swedish meatballs

Prep:10 mins **Cook:**25 mins plus cooling and chilling

Serves 4

Ingredients

- 2 tbsp rapeseed oil
- 1 onion , finely chopped
- 1 small garlic clove , finely grated
- 375g lean pork mince
- 1 medium egg yolk
- grating of nutmeg
- 50g fine fresh breadcrumbs
- 300ml hot low-salt beef stock
- ½ tbsp Dijon mustard
- 2 tbsp fat-free natural yogurt
- 400g spring greens , shredded
- lingonberry or cranberry sauce , to serve

Method

STEP 1

Put 1 tbsp rapeseed oil in a frying pan over a medium heat. Add the onion and fry for 10 mins or until soft and translucent. Add the garlic and cook for 1 min. Leave to cool.

STEP 2

Mix the cooled onions, pork mince, egg yolk, a good grating of nutmeg and the breadcrumbs in a bowl with your hands until well combined. Form into 12 balls and chill for 15 mins.

STEP 3

Heat the remaining oil in a frying pan and fry the meatballs for 5 mins over a medium heat, turning often until golden. Pour over the stock and bubble for 8-10 mins or until it has reduced a little. Stir through the mustard and yogurt.

STEP 4

Steam the greens for 5 mins or until tender. Serve the meatballs with the greens and a dollop of the sauce.

Singapore noodles with prawns

Prep:10 mins **Cook:**10 mins

Serves 2

Ingredients

- 2 nests thin vermicelli rice noodles
- 1 tbsp light soy sauce
- 1 tbsp oyster sauce
- 2 tsp mild curry powder
- 1 tbsp sesame oil
- 1 garlic clove , chopped
- 1 red chilli , thinly sliced (deseeded if you don't like it too hot)
- thumb-sized piece ginger , grated
- 1 medium onion , sliced
- 1 red pepper or yellow pepper, cut into thin batons
- 4 spring onions , cut in half lengthways then into batons
- 8 raw king prawns
- 1 large egg , beaten
- coriander leaves, to serve

Method

STEP 1

Soak the rice noodles in warm water for 5 mins until softened but still al dente. Drain and set aside.

STEP 2

In a small bowl, mix together the soy, oyster sauce and curry powder.

STEP 3

In a large wok, add half the oil and fry the garlic, chilli and ginger until golden, about 2 mins. Add the remaining oil, onion, pepper, spring onions, prawns and noodles and stir-fry for a few mins. Push everything to one side, add the egg and scramble. Add the soy sauce mixture, toss again for a few more mins, then remove from the heat. Sprinkle over the coriander leaves before serving.

Spiced carrot & lentil soup

Prep:10 mins **Cook:**15 mins

Serves 4

Ingredients

- 2 tsp cumin seeds
- pinch chilli flakes
- 2 tbsp olive oil
- 600g carrots, washed and coarsely grated (no need to peel)
- 140g split red lentils
- 1l hot vegetable stock (from a cube is fine)
- 125ml milk (to make it dairy-free, see 'try' below)
- plain yogurt and naan bread, to serve

Method

STEP 1

Heat a large saucepan and dry-fry 2 tsp cumin seeds and a pinch of chilli flakes for 1 min, or until they start to jump around the pan and release their aromas.

STEP 2

Scoop out about half with a spoon and set aside. Add 2 tbsp olive oil, 600g coarsely grated carrots, 140g split red lentils, 1l hot vegetable stock and 125ml milk to the pan and bring to the boil.

STEP 3

Simmer for 15 mins until the lentils have swollen and softened.

STEP 4

Whizz the soup with a stick blender or in a food processor until smooth (or leave it chunky if you prefer).

STEP 5

Season to taste and finish with a dollop of plain yogurt and a sprinkling of the reserved toasted spices. Serve with warmed naan breads.

Chana masala with pomegranate raita

Prep: 10 mins **Cook:** 35 mins

Serves 2

Ingredients

- 1 tbsp rapeseed oil
- 2 onions , halved and thinly sliced
- 1 tbsp chopped ginger
- 2 large garlic cloves , finely grated or crushed
- 1 green chilli , halved, deseeded and thinly sliced
- ½ tsp cumin seeds
- ½ tsp mustard seeds
- ½ tsp garam masala
- ½ tsp turmeric
- 1 tsp ground coriander
- 400g can chickpeas , undrained
- 4 small tomatoes (about 160g), cut into wedges
- 2 tsp vegetable bouillon powder
- cooked wholegrain rice , to serve (optional)

For the pomegranate raita

- 150ml plain bio yogurt
- 25g pomegranate seeds
- 2 tbsp finely chopped coriander , plus extra leaves to serve

Method

STEP 1

Heat the oil in a large non-stick pan, then cook the onions, ginger, garlic and chilli for 15-20 mins.

STEP 2

Add the spices, chickpeas, the liquid from the can, ¾ can cold water, the tomatoes and bouillon. Cover and simmer for 10 mins.

STEP 3

Meanwhile, mix the ingredients for the raita in a small bowl, reserving a few coriander leaves. Roughly mash some of the curry to thicken it. Spoon into bowls with rice, if you like. Scatter over the reserved coriander and serve with the raita on the side.

Leek, pea & watercress soup

Prep:10 mins **Cook:**22 mins

Serves 4

Ingredients

- 1 tbsp olive oil , plus a drizzle to serve
- 2 leeks , finely sliced
- 4 small garlic cloves , crushed
- 650-800ml hot veg stock
- 80g watercress
- 400g frozen peas
- 1 small lemon , zested and juiced
- small bunch of parsley , finely chopped
- dairy-free crème fraîche and crusty bread, to serve (optional)

Method

STEP 1

Heat the oil in a large saucepan over a medium heat. Add the leeks and garlic and fry for 7-10 mins or until softened and translucent.

STEP 2

Pour in the hot stock and simmer for 5-10 mins. Stir through the watercress, reserving a few leaves for garnish, then the peas, and cook for 5 mins until wilted. Use a hand blender or processor and whizz until smooth. Stir through the lemon juice and zest, then season to taste.

Stir through half the parsley. Ladle into bowls and top with the remaining parsley, reserved watercress and a drizzle of olive oil. Swirl through some crème fraîche, then serve with crusty bread, if you like.

Slow cooker lasagne

Prep:1 hr and 15 mins **Cook:**3 hrs

Serves 4

Ingredients

- 2 tsp rapeseed oil
- 2 onions, finely chopped
- 4 celery sticks (about 175g), finely diced
- 4 carrots (320g), finely diced
- 2 garlic cloves, chopped
- 400g lean (5% fat) mince beef
- 400g can chopped tomatoes
- 2 tbsp tomato purée
- 2 tsp vegetable bouillon
- 1 tbsp balsamic vinegar
- 1 tbsp fresh thyme leaves
- 6 wholewheat lasagne sheets (105g)

For the sauce

- 400ml whole milk
- 50g wholemeal flour
- 1 bay leaf
- generous grating of nutmeg
- 15g finely grated parmesan

Method

STEP 1

Heat the slow cooker if necessary. Heat the oil in a large non-stick pan and fry the onions, celery, carrots and garlic for 5-10 mins, stirring frequently until softened and starting to colour. Tip in the meat and break it down with a wooden spoon, stirring until it browns. Pour in the tomatoes with a quarter of a can of water, the tomato purée, bouillon, balsamic vinegar, thyme and plenty of black pepper, return to the boil and cook for 5 mins more.

STEP 2

Spoon half the mince in the slow cooker and top with half the lasagne, breaking it where necessary so it covers as much of the meat layer as possible. Top with the rest of the meat, and then another layer of the lasagne. Cover and cook on Low while you make the sauce.

STEP 3

Tip the milk and flour into a pan with the bay leaf and nutmeg and cook on the hob, whisking continuously until thickened. Carry on cooking for a few mins to cook the flour. Remove the bay leaf and stir in the cheese. Pour onto the pasta and spread out with a spatula, then cover and cook for 3 hours until the meat is cooked and the pasta is tender. Allow to settle for 10 mins before serving with salad.

Cauliflower rice

Prep:3 mins **Cook:**7 mins

Serves 4

Ingredients

- 1 medium cauliflower
- good handful coriander, chopped
- cumin seeds, toasted (optional)

Method

STEP 1

Cut the hard core and stalks from the cauliflower and pulse the rest in a food processor to make grains the size of rice. Tip into a heatproof bowl, cover with cling film, then pierce and microwave for 7 mins on High – there is no need to add any water. Stir in the coriander. For spicier rice, add some toasted cumin seeds.

Italian borlotti bean, pumpkin & farro soup

Prep:15 mins **Cook:**35 mins

Serves 6

Ingredients

- 4 tbsp extra virgin olive oil , plus extra to serve
- 1 onion , fincly chopped
- 1 celery stick , cut into chunks
- 750g pumpkin or squash, peeled, deseeded and cut into small chunks
- 1 carrot , peeled and cut into chunks
- 3 garlic cloves , chopped
- 3 tbsp tomato purée
- 1.2l chicken stock or vegetable stock
- 75g farro or mixed grains (such as barley or spelt)
- 50-80g parmesan rinds or vegetarian alternative (optional), plus a few shavings to serve
- 400g can borlotti beans , drained
- 2 handfuls baby spinach
- 2 tbsp chopped parsley or 8 whole sage leaves

Method

STEP 1

Heat the oil in a heavy-bottomed saucepan. Add the onion, celery, pumpkin or squash and carrot and cook until the vegetables have some colour. Add a splash of water and some seasoning, then cover the pan and let the vegetables cook over a very low heat for 5 mins.

STEP 2

Add the garlic and cook for another couple of mins, then add the tomato purée, stock, mixed grains, parmesan rinds, if using, and some seasoning. Simmer for about 15 mins (or until the grains are cooked), adding the beans for the final 5 mins. In the last few mins, add the spinach, then taste for seasoning.

STEP 3

If you want to use sage, fry the leaves whole in a little olive oil before adding to the soup. If you prefer to use parsley, you can just add it directly to the soup. Serve with shavings of parmesan and a drizzle of extra virgin olive oil on top of each bowlful. Remove the parmesan rinds and serve.

Asparagus & new potato frittata

Prep: 10 mins **Cook:** 12 mins

Serves 3

Ingredients

- 200g new potatoes, quartered
- 100g asparagus tips
- 1 tbsp olive oil
- 1 onion, finely chopped
- 6 eggs, beaten
- 40g cheddar, grated
- rocket or mixed leaves, to serve

Method

STEP 1

Heat the grill to high. Put the potatoes in a pan of cold salted water and bring to the boil. Once boiling, cook for 4-5 mins until nearly tender, then add the asparagus for a final 1 min. Drain.

STEP 2

Meanwhile, heat the oil in an ovenproof frying pan and add the onion. Cook for about 8 mins until softened.

STEP 3

Mix the eggs with half the cheese in a jug and season well. Pour over the onion in the pan, then scatter over the asparagus and potatoes. Top with the remaining cheese and put under the grill for 5 mins or until golden and cooked through. Cut into wedges and serve from the pan with salad.

Moroccan roast lamb with roasted roots & coriander

Prep: 15 mins **Cook:** 55 mins

Serves 4

Ingredients

- ½ leg of lamb , around 800g
- 2 red onions , cut into wedges
- 1 butternut squash , skin left on, cut into wedges
- 1 celeriac , peeled and cut into wedges
- 2½ tbsp cold pressed rapeseed oil
- 2 tbsp ras el hanout
- 8 garlic cloves , skin on
- 1 small bunch coriander
- ½ tsp cumin seeds
- 1 lemon , zested and juiced
- 1/2 green chilli , deseeded

Method

STEP 1

Take the lamb out of the fridge while you chop the onions, squash and celeriac. Heat oven to 200C/180C fan/gas 6. Trim any excess fat off the leg of lamb, then cut a few slashes into the meat. Rub ½ tbsp oil and 1 tbsp ras el hanout over the lamb and season with salt and pepper. Put the onion, celeriac, butternut squash into a large roasting tin with the garlic. Toss with the remaining ras el hanout, remaining oil and some salt and pepper. Nestle the lamb into the tin and put in the oven to roast for 40 mins.

STEP 2

Take the lamb out of the oven and leave to rest. Put the veg back in the oven for 20 mins. Meanwhile, blitz the coriander, cumin seeds, lemon zest, lemon juice and green chilli together in a mini food processor until finely chopped and vivid green.

STEP 3

Carve the lamb, put on a platter, then pile on the veg. Sprinkle over some of the coriander mixture before taking the platter to the table for everyone to help themselves.

Little spicy veggie pies

Prep:10 mins **Cook:**55 mins

Serves 4

Ingredients

- 2 tbsp rapeseed oil
- 2 tbsp finely chopped ginger
- 3 tbsp Korma curry powder
- 3 large garlic cloves , grated
- 2 x 400g cans chickpeas , undrained
- 320g carrots , coarsely grated
- 160g frozen sweetcorn
- 1 tbsp vegetable bouillon powder
- 4 tbsp tomato purée
- 250g bag spinach , cooked

For the topping

- 750g potatoes , peeled and cut into 3cm chunks
- 1 tsp ground coriander
- 10g fresh coriander , chopped
- 150g coconut yogurt

Method

STEP 1

To make the topping, boil the potatoes for 15-20 mins until tender then drain, reserving the water, and mash with the ground and fresh coriander and yogurt until creamy.

STEP 2

While the potatoes are boiling, heat the oil in a large pan, add the ginger and fry briefly, tip in the curry powder and garlic, stirring quickly as you don't want it to burn, then tip in a can of chickpeas with the water from the can. Stir well, then mash in the pan to smash them up a bit, then tip in the second can of chickpeas, again with the water from the can, along with the carrots, corn, bouillon and tomato purée. Simmer for 5-10 mins, adding some of the potato water, if needed, to loosen.

STEP 3

Heat the oven to 200C/180C fan/gas 6. Spoon the filling into four individual pie dishes (each about 10cm wide, 8cm deep) and top with the mash, smoothing it to seal round the edges of the dishes. If you're following our Healthy Diet Plan, bake two for 25 mins until golden, and cook half the spinach, saving the rest of the bag for another day. Cover and chill the remaining two pies to eat another day. Will keep in the fridge for four days. If freezing, to reheat, bake from frozen for 40-45 mins until golden and piping hot.

Cashew curry

Prep: 20 mins **Cook:** 1 hr

Serves 3

Ingredients

- 1 small onion , chopped
- 3-4 garlic cloves
- thumb-sized piece ginger , peeled and roughly chopped
- 3 green chillies , deseeded
- small pack coriander , leaves picked and stalk roughly chopped
- 100g unsalted cashews
- 2 tbsp coconut oil
- 1 ½ tbsp garam masala
- 400g can chopped tomatoes
- 450ml chicken stock
- 3 large chicken breasts (about 475g), any visible fat removed, chopped into chunks
- 155g fat-free Greek yogurt
- 10ml single cream (optional)

To serve

- 165g boiled or steamed greens (choose from spinach, kale, runner beans, asparagus or broccoli)

Method

STEP 1

Put the onion, garlic, ginger, chillies and coriander stalks in a small food processor and blitz to a paste.

STEP 2

Heat a large, non-stick frying pan over a medium heat. Add the cashews and toast for 1-2 mins until light golden. Set aside and return the pan to the heat. Add the oil and stir-fry the paste for 5 mins to soften. Add the garam masala and cook for a further 2 mins.

STEP 3

Add the tomatoes and stock to the pan. Mix well, then tip into a blender with the cashews and blitz until smooth. Return to the pan, season and bring to the boil, then lower to a simmer.

STEP 4

Cook for 30 mins until the sauce has thickened then add the chicken, cover with a lid and simmer for another 15 mins, until the chicken is cooked through. Add the yogurt and cream (if using), and stir well to make a creamy sauce.

STEP 5

Scatter with the coriander leaves and serve with the greens.

Harissa-crumbed fish with lentils & peppers

Prep:15 mins **Cook:**15 mins

Serves 4

Ingredients

- 2 x 200g pouches cooked puy lentils
- 200g jar roasted red peppers , drained and torn into chunks
- 50g black olives , from a jar, roughly chopped
- 1 lemon , zested and cut into wedges
- 3 tbsp olive or rapeseed oil
- 4 x 140g cod fillets (or another white fish)
- 100g fresh breadcrumbs
- 1 tbsp harissa
- ½ small pack flat-leaf parsley , chopped

Method

STEP 1

Heat oven to 200C/180C fan/gas 6. Mix the lentils, peppers, olives, lemon zest, 2 tbsp oil and some seasoning in a roasting tin. Top with the fish fillets. Mix the breadcrumbs, harissa and the remaining oil and put a few spoonfuls on top of each piece of fish. Bake for 12-15 mins until the fish is cooked, the topping is crispy and the lentils are hot. Scatter with the parsley and squeeze over the lemon wedges.

Ginger, sesame and chilli prawn & broccoli stir-fry

Prep:5 mins **Cook:**10 mins

Serves 2

Ingredients

- 250g broccoli , thin-stemmed if you like, cut into even-sized florets
- 2 balls stem ginger , finely chopped, plus 2 tbsp syrup from the jar
- 3 tbsp low-salt soy sauce
- 1 garlic clove , crushed
- 1 red chilli , a little thinly sliced, the rest deseeded and finely chopped
- 2 tsp sesame seeds
- ½ tbsp sesame oil
- 200g raw king prawns
- 100g beansprouts
- cooked rice or noodles, to serve

Method

STEP 1

Heat a pan of water until boiling. Tip in the broccoli and cook for just 1 min – it should still have a good crunch. Meanwhile, mix the stem ginger and syrup, soy sauce, garlic and finely chopped chilli.

STEP 2

Toast the sesame seeds in a dry wok or large frying pan. When they're nicely browned, turn up the heat and add the oil, prawns and cooked broccoli. Stir-fry for a few mins until the prawns turn pink. Pour over the ginger sauce, then tip in the beansprouts. Cook for 30 seconds, or until the beansprouts are heated thoroughly, adding a splash more soy or ginger syrup, if you like. Scatter with the sliced chilli and serve over rice or noodles.

Turkey meatloaf

Prep:15 mins **Cook:**55 mins

Serves 4

Ingredients

- 1 tbsp olive oil
- 1 large onion , finely chopped
- 1 garlic clove , crushed
- 2 tbsp Worcestershire sauce
- 2 tsp tomato purée , plus 1 tbsp for the beans
- 500g turkey mince (thigh is best)
- 1 large egg , beaten
- 85g fresh white breadcrumbs
- 2 tbsp barbecue sauce , plus 4 tbsp for the beans
- 2 x 400g cans cannellini beans
- 1-2 tbsp roughly chopped parsley

Method

STEP 1

Heat oven to 180C/160C fan/gas 4. Heat the oil in a large frying pan and cook the onion for 8-10 mins until softened. Add the garlic, Worcestershire sauce and 2 tsp tomato purée, and stir until combined. Set aside to cool.

STEP 2

Put the turkey mince, egg, breadcrumbs and cooled onion mix in a large bowl and season well. Mix everything to combine, then shape into a rectangular loaf and place in a large roasting tin. Spread 2 tbsp barbecue sauce over the meatloaf and bake for 30 mins.

STEP 3

Meanwhile, drain 1 can of beans only, then pour both cans into a large bowl. Add the remaining barbecue sauce and tomato purée. Season and set aside.

STEP 4

When the meatloaf has had its initial cooking time, scatter the beans around the outside and bake for 15 mins more until the meatloaf is cooked through and the beans are piping hot. Scatter over the parsley and serve the meatloaf in slices.

Paneer jalfrezi with cumin rice

Prep: 20 mins **Cook:** 30 mins

Serves 4

Ingredients

- 2 tsp cold-pressed rapeseed oil
- 1 large and 1 medium onion , large one finely chopped and medium one cut into wedges
- 2 large garlic cloves , chopped
- 50g ginger , peeled and shredded
- 2 tsp ground coriander
- 2 tsp cumin seeds
- 400g can chopped tomatoes
- 1 tbsp vegetable bouillon powder
- 135g paneer , chopped
- 2 large peppers , seeded and chopped
- 1 red or green chilli , deseeded and sliced
- 25g coriander , chopped

For the rice

- 260g brown basmati rice
- 1 tsp cumin seeds

Method

STEP 1

Heat 1 tsp oil a large non-stick frying pan and fry the chopped onions, garlic and half the ginger for 5 mins until softened. Add the ground coriander and cumin seeds and cook for 1 min more, then tip in the tomatoes, half a can of water and the bouillon. Blitz everything together with a stick blender until very smooth, then bring to a simmer. Cover and cook for 15 mins.

STEP 2

Meanwhile, cook the rice and cumin seeds in a pan of boiling water for 25 mins, or until tender.

STEP 3

Heat the remaining oil in a non-stick wok and fry the paneer until lightly coloured. Remove from the pan and set aside. Add the peppers, onion wedges and chilli to the pan and stir-fry until the veg is tender, but still retains some bite. Mix the stir-fried veg and paneer into the sauce with the chopped coriander, then serve with the rice. If you're following our Healthy Diet Plan, eat two portions of the curry and rice, then chill the rest for another day. Will keep for up to three days, covered, in the fridge. To serve on the second night, reheat the leftover portions in the microwave until piping hot.

Low 'n' slow rib steak with Cuban mojo salsa

Prep: 20 mins **Cook:** 3 hrs and 20 mins

Serves 2

Ingredients

- 1 rib steak on the bone or côte du boeuf (about 800g)
- 1 tbsp rapeseed oil
- 1 garlic clove
- 2 thyme sprigs
- 25g butter , chopped into small pieces
- sweet potato fries
- a dressed salad , to serve

For the mojo salsa

- 2 limes
- 1 small orange
- ½ small bunch mint , finely chopped
- small bunch coriander , finely chopped
- 4 spring onions , finely chopped
- 1 small garlic clove , crushed
- 1 fat green chilli , finely chopped
- 4 tbsp extra virgin rapeseed oil or olive oil

Method

STEP 1

Leave the beef at room temperature for about 1 hr before you cook it. Heat oven to 60C/40C fan/gas 1 /4 if you like your beef medium rare, or 65C/45C fan/gas 1 /4 for medium. (Cooking at these low temperatures will be more accurate in an electric oven than in a gas one. If using gas, put the oven on the lowest setting you have, and be aware that the cooking time may be shorter.)

STEP 2

Put the unseasoned beef in a heavy-based ovenproof frying pan. Cook in the middle of the oven for 3 hrs undisturbed.

STEP 3

Meanwhile, make the salsa. Zest the limes and orange into a bowl. Cut each in half and place, cut-side down, in a hot pan. Cook for a few mins until the fruits are charred, then squeeze the juice into the bowl. Add the other ingredients and season well.

STEP 4

When the beef is cooked, it should look dry on the surface, and dark pink in colour. If you have a meat thermometer, test the internal temperature – it should be 58-60C. Remove the pan from the oven and set over a high heat on the hob. Add the oil and sear the meat on both sides for a few mins until caramelised. Sear the fat for a few mins too. Smash the garlic clove with the heel of your hand and add this to the pan with the thyme and butter. When the butter is foaming, spoon it over the beef and cook for another 1-2 mins. Transfer the beef to a warm plate, cover with foil, and leave to rest for 5-10 mins. Carve away from the bone and into slices before serving with the salsa, fries and salad.

Asparagus & broad bean lasagne

Prep:35 mins **Cook:**1 hr and 10 mins

Serves 4

Ingredients

- 225ml whole milk
- 320g frozen baby broad beans
- 3 garlic cloves , chopped

- 30g pack fresh basil , roughly chopped
- ½ lemon , zested
- 4 spring onions , chopped
- 1 tsp vegetable bouillon powder
- 6 wholemeal lasagne sheets
- 320g frozen peas
- 2 x 300g tubs low-fat cottage cheese
- 1 egg
- whole nutmeg , for grating
- 250g asparagus , woody ends trimmed
- 25g parmesan or vegetarian alternative, finely grated

Method

STEP 1

Heat oven to 180C/160C fan/gas 4. Heat the milk in a pan until just boiling, then tip in the beans (add a splash of water to cover if you need to). Cook for 3 mins to defrost, then add the garlic, basil, lemon zest, spring onions and bouillon, then blitz for a few mins with a hand blender until smooth.

STEP 2

Spoon half the purée into a 20 x 26cm ovenproof dish. Top with 3 lasagne sheets, the remaining purée, and the peas, then the remaining lasagne sheets.

STEP 3

Whisk the cottage cheese with the egg and a good grating of nutmeg. Pour over the lasagne, then press in the asparagus and scatter over the parmesan. Bake for 1 hr until golden and a knife easily slides through. Can be kept chilled for two days.

Smoky chickpeas on toast

Prep:2 mins Cook:10 mins

Serves 2

Ingredients

- 1 tsp olive oil or vegetable oil, plus a drizzle

- 1 small onion or banana shallot, chopped
- 2 tsp chipotle paste
- 250ml passata
- 400g can chickpeas , drained
- 2 tsp honey
- 2 tsp red wine vinegar
- 2-4 slices good crusty bread
- 2 eggs

Method

STEP 1

Heat ½ tsp of the oil in a pan. Tip in the onion and cook until soft, about 5-8 mins, then add the chipotle paste, passata, chickpeas, honey and vinegar. Season and bubble for 5 mins.

STEP 2

Toast the bread. Heat the remaining oil in a frying pan and fry the eggs. Drizzle the toast with a little oil, then top with the chickpeas and fried eggs.

Fennel spaghetti

Prep:15 mins **Cook:**30 mins

Serves 2

Ingredients

- 1 tbsp olive oil , plus extra for serving
- 1 tsp fennel seeds
- 2 small garlic cloves , 1 crushed, 1 thinly sliced
- 1 lemon , zested and juiced
- 1 fennel bulb , finely sliced, fronds reserved
- 150g spaghetti
- ½ pack flat-leaf parsley , chopped
- shaved parmesan (or vegetarian alternative), to serve (optional)

Method

STEP 1

Heat the oil in a frying pan over a medium heat and cook the fennel seeds until they pop. Sizzle the garlic for 1 min, then add the lemon zest and half the fennel slices. Cook for 10-12 mins or until the fennel has softened.

STEP 2

Meanwhile, bring a pan of salted water to the boil and cook the pasta for 1 min less than pack instructions. Use tongs to transfer the pasta to the frying pan along with a good splash of pasta water. Increase the heat to high and toss well. Stir through the remaining fennel slices, the parsley and lemon juice, season generously, then tip straight into two bowls to serve. Top with the fennel fronds, extra olive oil and parmesan shavings, if you like.

Healthy bolognese

Prep:5 mins **Cook:**20 mins

2 generously, 4 as a snack

Ingredients

- 100g wholewheat linguine
- 2 tsp rapeseed oil
- 1 fennel bulb , finely chopped
- 2 garlic cloves , sliced
- 200g pork mince with less than 5% fat
- 200g whole cherry tomatoes
- 1 tbsp balsamic vinegar
- 1 tsp vegetable bouillon powder
- generous handful chopped basil

Method

STEP 1

Bring a large pan of water to the boil, then cook the linguine following pack instructions, about 10 mins.

STEP 2

Meanwhile, heat the oil in a non-stick wok or wide pan. Add the fennel and garlic and cook, stirring every now and then, until tender, about 10 mins.

STEP 3

Tip in the pork and stir-fry until it changes colour, breaking it up as you go so there are no large clumps. Add the tomatoes, vinegar and bouillon, then cover the pan and cook for 10 mins over a low heat until the tomatoes burst and the pork is cooked and tender. Add the linguine and basil and plenty of pepper, and toss well before serving.

Vietnamese chicken noodle soup

Prep: 20 mins **Cook:** 25 mins

Serves 6

Ingredients

- 1 tbsp vegetable oil
- 3 shallots, sliced
- 3 garlic cloves, sliced
- 1 lemongrass stalk, chopped
- 2.5cm piece ginger, sliced
- 3 star anise
- 1 cinnamon stick
- 1 tsp coriander seeds
- ¼ tsp Chinese five spice
- ¼ tsp black peppercorns
- 1 tsp caster sugar
- 1 tbsp fish sauce
- 1.25 - 1.5 litres good quality fresh chicken stock
- 3 large chicken breasts (about 500g)

To serve

- 450g rice noodles
- 4 spring onions, finely sliced on an angle
- 1 carrot, shredded or peeled into ribbon with a vegetable peeler
- 2 large handfuls (150g) mung bean sprouts

- large bunch coriander, chopped
- small bunch mint, leaves chopped
- 1 red chilli, thinly sliced (optional)
- 2 tbsp crispy fried shallots (optional)
- 1 kaffir lime leaf, tough central stalk removed, very finely sliced, (optional)
- 1 lime, cut into wedges

Method

STEP 1

Heat the oil in a small frying pan on medium heat and gently cook the shallots and garlic until caramelised and golden brown (about 4-5 mins).

STEP 2

In a large saucepan, add the caramelised shallots and garlic, lemongrass, ginger, star anise, cinnamon stick, coriander seeds, Chinese five-spice, peppercorns, sugar, fish sauce, chicken stock and chicken breasts. Cover with a lid and bring to a very gentle simmer for about 15 mins.

STEP 3

Meanwhile, cook the noodles, following pack instructions, until just cooked through (do not over-cook). Rinse under cold water to prevent them sticking together. Drain and divide between serving bowls.

STEP 4

Strain the soup through a sieve. Discard the spices. Shred the chicken and keep to one side. Return soup to the pot and bring to a boil. Season to taste with more fish sauce if needed.

STEP 5

To serve, ladle piping hot soup into bowls of noodles and chicken, and top with spring onion, carrot, bean sprouts, and herbs, plus the chilli, crispy shallots and kaffir lime leaf if using. Serve with a lime wedge to squeeze over, and more fish sauce and chilli to taste.

Broccoli pasta shells

Prep: 5 mins **Cook:** 15 mins

Serves 4

Ingredients

- 1 head of broccoli, chopped into florets
- 1 garlic clove, unpeeled
- 2 tbsp olive oil
- 250g pasta shells
- ½ small pack parsley
- ½ small pack basil
- 30g toasted pine nuts
- ½ lemon, zested and juiced
- 30g parmesan (or vegetarian alternative), plus extra to serve

Method

STEP 1

Heat the oven to 200C/180C fan/gas 6. Toss the broccoli and garlic in 1 tbsp of the olive oil on a roasting tray and roast in the oven for 10-12 mins, until softened.

STEP 2

Tip the pasta shells into a pan of boiling, salted water. Cook according to packet instructions and drain. Tip the parsley, basil, pine nuts, lemon juice and parmesan into a blender. Once the broccoli is done, set aside a few of the smaller pieces. Squeeze the garlic from its skin, add to the blender along with the rest of the broccoli, pulse to a pesto and season well.

STEP 3

Toss the pasta with the pesto. Add the reserved broccoli florets, split between two bowls and top with a little extra parmesan, the lemon zest and a good grinding of black pepper, if you like.

Chilli chicken wraps

Prep:10 mins **Cook:**25 mins

Serves 4

Ingredients

- 2 tbsp vegetable oil
- 6 boneless, skinless chicken thighs, cut into bite-sized pieces

- 1 large onion, thinly sliced into half-moons
- 2 garlic cloves, finely chopped
- 3cm piece ginger, peeled and finely chopped
- ½ tsp ground cumin
- ½ tsp garam masala
- 1 tbsp tomato purée
- 1 red chilli, thinly sliced into rings
- juice ½ lemon
- 4 rotis, warmed
- ½ small red onion, chopped
- 4 tbsp mango chutney or lime pickle
- 4 handfuls mint or coriander
- 4 tbsp yogurt

Method

STEP 1

Heat the oil in a large frying pan over a medium heat. Add the chicken, brown on all sides, then remove. Add the onion, garlic, ginger and a pinch of salt. Cook for 5 mins or until softened.

STEP 2

Increase the heat to high. Return the chicken to the pan with the spices, tomato purée, chilli and lemon juice. Season well and cook for 10 mins or until the chicken is tender.

STEP 3

Divide the chicken, red onion, chutney, herbs and yogurt between the four warm rotis. Roll up and serve with plenty of napkins

Squash & spinach fusilli with pecans

Prep: 10 mins **Cook:** 40 mins

Serves 2

Ingredients

- 160g butternut squash , diced
- 3 garlic cloves , sliced

- 1 tbsp chopped sage leaves
- 2 tsp rapeseed oil
- 1 large courgette , halved and sliced
- 6 pecan halves
- 115g wholemeal fusilli
- 125g bag baby spinach

Method

STEP 1

Heat oven to 200C/180C fan/gas 6. Toss the butternut squash, garlic and sage in the oil, then spread out in a roasting tin and cook in the oven for 20 mins, add the courgettes and cook for a further 15 mins. Give everything a stir, then add the pecans and cook for 5 mins more until the nuts are toasted and the vegetables are tender and starting to caramelise.

STEP 2

Meanwhile, boil the pasta according to pack instructions – about 12 mins. Drain, then tip into a serving bowl and toss with the spinach so that it wilts in the heat from the pasta. Add the roasted veg and pecans, breaking up the nuts a little, and toss again really well before serving.

Asparagus & lemon spaghetti with peas

Prep:7 mins **Cook:**12 mins

Serves 2

Ingredients

- 150g wholemeal spaghetti
- 160g asparagus, ends trimmed and cut into lengths
- 2 tbsp rapeseed oil
- 2 leeks (220g), cut into lengths, then thin strips
- 1 red chilli, deseeded and finely chopped
- 1 garlic clove, finely grated
- 160g frozen peas
- 1 lemon, zested and juiced, plus wedges to serve

Method

STEP 1

Boil the spaghetti for 12 mins until al dente, adding the asparagus for the last 3 mins. Meanwhile, heat the oil in a large non-stick frying pan, add the leeks and chilli and cook for 5 mins. Stir in the garlic, peas and lemon zest and juice and cook for a few mins more.

STEP 2

Drain and add the pasta to the pan with ¼ mug of the pasta water and toss everything together until well mixed. Spoon into shallow bowls and serve with lemon wedges for squeezing over, if you like.

Low-fat moussaka

Prep: 15 mins **Cook:** 40 mins

Serves 4

Ingredients

- 200g frozen sliced peppers
- 3 garlic cloves , crushed
- 200g extra-lean minced beef
- 100g red lentils
- 2 tsp dried oregano , plus extra for sprinkling
- 500ml carton passata
- 1 aubergine , sliced into 1.5cm rounds
- 4 tomatoes , sliced into 1cm rounds
- 2 tsp olive oil
- 25g parmesan , finely grated
- 170g pot 0% fat Greek yogurt
- freshly grated nutmeg

Method

STEP 1

Cook the peppers gently in a large non-stick pan for about 5 mins – the water from them should stop them sticking. Add the garlic and cook for 1 min more, then add the beef, breaking up with a fork, and cook until brown. Tip in the lentils, half the oregano, the passata and a splash of water. Simmer for 15-20 mins until the lentils are tender, adding more water if you need to.

STEP 2

Meanwhile, heat the grill to Medium. Arrange the aubergine and tomato slices on a non-stick baking tray and brush with the oil. Sprinkle with the remaining oregano and some seasoning, then grill for 1-2 mins each side until lightly charred – you may need to do this in batches.

STEP 3

Mix half the Parmesan with the yogurt and some seasoning. Divide the beef mixture between 4 small ovenproof dishes and top with the sliced aubergine and tomato. Spoon over the yogurt topping and sprinkle with the extra oregano, Parmesan and nutmeg. Grill for 3-4 mins until bubbling. Serve with a salad, if you like.

Courgette, leek & goat's cheese soup

Prep:8 mins **Cook:**17 mins

Serves 4

Ingredients

- 1 tbsp rapeseed oil
- 400g leeks, well washed and sliced
- 450g courgettes, sliced
- 3 tsp vegetable bouillon powder, made up to 1 litre with boiling water
- 400g spinach
- 150g tub soft vegetarian goat's cheese
- 15g basil, plus a few leaves to serve
- 8 tsp omega seed mix (see tip)
- 4 x 25g portions wholegrain rye bread

Method

STEP 1

Heat the oil in a large pan and fry the leeks for a few mins to soften. Add the courgettes, then cover the pan and cook for 5 mins more. Pour in the stock, cover and cook for about 7 mins.

STEP 2

Add the spinach, then cover the pan and cook for 5 mins so that it wilts. Take off the heat and blitz until really smooth with a hand blender. Add the goat's cheese and basil, then blitz again.

STEP 3

If you're making this recipe as part of our two-person Summer Healthy Diet Plan, spoon half the soup into two bowls or large flasks, then cool and chill the remainder for another day. Reheat in a pan or microwave to serve. If serving in bowls, scatter with some extra basil leaves and the seeds, and eat with the rye bread.

Salmon salad with sesame dressing

Prep:7 mins **Cook:**16 mins

Serves 2

Ingredients

For the salad

- 250g new potatoes , sliced
- 160g French beans , trimmed
- 2 wild salmon fillets
- 80g salad leaves
- 4 small clementines , 3 sliced, 1 juiced
- handful of basil , chopped
- handful of coriander , chopped

For the dressing

- 2 tsp sesame oil
- 2 tsp tamari
- ½ lemon , juiced
- 1 red chilli , deseeded and chopped
- 2 tbsp finely chopped onion (1/4 small onion)

Method

STEP 1

Steam the potatoes and beans in a steamer basket set over a pan of boiling water for 8 mins. Arrange the salmon fillets on top and steam for a further 6-8 mins, or until the salmon flakes easily when tested with a fork.

STEP 2

Meanwhile, mix the dressing ingredients together along with the clementine juice. If eating straightaway, divide the salad leaves between two plates and top with the warm potatoes and beans and the clementine slices. Arrange the salmon fillets on top, scatter over the herbs and spoon over the dressing. If taking to work, prepare the potatoes, beans and salmon the night before, then pack into a rigid airtight container with the salad leaves kept separate. Put the salad elements together and dress just before eating to prevent the leaves from wilting.

Ginger chicken & green bean noodles

Prep:10 mins **Cook:**15 mins

Serves 2

Ingredients

- ½ tbsp vegetable oil
- 2 skinless chicken breasts, sliced
- 200g green beans , trimmed and halved crosswise
- thumb-sized piece of ginger , peeled and cut into matchsticks
- 2 garlic cloves , sliced
- 1 ball stem ginger , finely sliced, plus 1 tsp syrup from the jar
- 1 tsp cornflour , mixed with 1 tbsp water
- 1 tsp dark soy sauce , plus extra to serve (optional)
- 2 tsp rice vinegar
- 200g cooked egg noodles

Method

STEP 1

Heat the oil in a wok over a high heat and stir-fry the chicken for 5 mins. Add the green beans and stir-fry for 4-5 mins more until the green beans are just tender, and the chicken is just cooked through.

STEP 2

Stir in the fresh ginger and garlic, and stir-fry for 2 mins, then add the stem ginger and syrup, the cornflour mix, soy sauce and vinegar. Stir-fry for 1 min, then toss in the noodles. Cook until everything is hot and the sauce coats the noodles. Drizzle with more soy, if you like, and serve.

Potato, pea & egg curry rotis

Prep:5 mins **Cook:**25 mins

Serves 4

Ingredients

- 1 tbsp oil
- 2 tbsp mild curry paste
- 400g can chopped tomatoes
- 2 potatoes , cut into small chunks
- 200g peas
- 3 eggs , hard-boiled
- pack rotis , warmed through
- 150g tub natural yogurt , to serve

Method

STEP 1

Heat the oil in a saucepan and briefly fry the curry paste. Tip in the tomatoes and half a can of water and bring to a simmer. Add the potatoes and cook for 20 mins, or until the potato is tender. Stir in the peas and cook for 3 mins.

STEP 2

Halve the eggs and place them on top of the curry, then warm everything through. Serve with the rotis and yogurt on the side.

Thai prawn & ginger noodles

Prep:15 mins **Cook:**15 mins plus soaking

Serves 2

Ingredients

- 100g folded rice noodles (sen lek)
- zest and juice 1 small orange
- 1½-2 tbsp red curry paste
- 1-2 tsp fish sauce
- 2 tsp light brown soft sugar
- 1 tbsp sunflower oil
- 25g ginger, scraped and shredded
- 2 large garlic cloves, sliced
- 1 red pepper, deseeded and sliced
- 85g sugar snap peas, halved lengthways
- 140g beansprouts
- 175g pack raw king prawns
- handful chopped basil
- handful chopped coriander

Method

STEP 1

Put the noodles in a bowl and pour over boiling water to cover them. Set aside to soak for 10 mins. Stir together the orange juice and zest, curry paste, fish sauce, sugar and 3 tbsp water to make a sauce.

STEP 2

Heat the oil in a large wok and add half the ginger and the garlic. Cook, stirring, for 1 min. Add the pepper and stir-fry for 3 mins more. Toss in the sugar snaps, cook briefly, then pour in the curry sauce. Add the beansprouts and prawns, and continue cooking until the prawns just turn pink. Drain the noodles, then toss these into the pan with the herbs and remaining ginger. Mix until the noodles are well coated in the sauce, then serve.

Easy soup maker lentil soup

Prep:5 mins **Cook:**30 mins

Serves 4

Ingredients

- 750ml vegetable or ham stock
- 75g red lentils
- 3 carrots , finely chopped
- 1 medium leek , sliced (150g)
- small handful chopped parsley , to serve

Method

STEP 1

Put the stock, lentils, carrots and leek into a soup maker, and press the 'chunky soup' function. Make sure you don't fill it above the max fill line. The soup will look a little foamy to start, but don't worry – it will disappear once cooked.

STEP 2

Once the cycle is complete, check the lentils are tender, and season well. Scatter over the parsley to serve.

Cod with cucumber, avocado & mango salsa salad

Prep:5 mins **Cook:**8 mins

Serves 2

Ingredients

- 2 x skinless cod fillets
- 1 lime , zested and juiced
- 1 small mango , peeled, stoned and chopped (or 2 peaches, stoned and chopped)
- 1 small avocado , stoned, peeled and sliced
- ¼ cucumber , chopped
- 160g cherry tomatoes , quartered
- 1 red chilli , deseeded and chopped
- 2 spring onions , sliced
- handful chopped coriander

Method

STEP 1

Heat oven to 200C/180C fan/gas 6. Put the fish in a shallow ovenproof dish and pour over half the lime juice, with a little of the zest, then grind over some black pepper. Bake for 8 mins or until the fish flakes easily but is still moist.

STEP 2

Meanwhile, put the rest of the ingredients, plus the remaining lime juice and zest, in a bowl and combine well. Spoon onto plates and top with the cod, spooning over any juices in the dish.

Slow cooker mushroom risotto

Prep:30 mins **Cook:**1 hr

Serves 4

Ingredients

- 1 onion, finely chopped
- 1 tsp olive oil
- 250g chestnut mushrooms, sliced
- 1l vegetable stock
- 50g porcini
- 300g wholegrain rice
- small bunch parsley, finely chopped
- grated vegetarian parmesan-style cheese to serve

Method

STEP 1

Heat the slow cooker if necessary. Fry the onion in the oil in a frying pan with a splash of water for 10 minutes or until it is soft but not coloured. Add the mushroom slices and stir them around until they start to soften and release their juices.

STEP 2

Meanwhile pour the stock into a saucepan and add the porcini, bring to a simmer and then leave to soak. Tip the onions and mushrooms into the slow cooker and add the rice, stir it in well.

Pour over the stock and porcini leaving any bits of sediment in the saucepan (or pour the mixture through a fine sieve).

STEP 3

Cook on High for 3 hours, stirring halfway. and then check the consistency – the rice should be cooked. If it needs a little more liquid stir in a splash of stock. Stir in the parsley and season. Serve with the parmesan.

Home-style pork curry with cauliflower rice

Prep: 15 mins **Cook:** 1 hr

Serves 4

Ingredients

For the curry

- 425g lean pork fillet (tenderloin), cubed
- 2 tbsp Madras curry powder
- 2 tbsp red wine vinegar
- 1 tbsp rapeseed oil
- 1 large onion , finely chopped
- 2 tbsp finely shredded ginger
- 1 tsp fennel , toasted in a pan then crushed
- 1 tsp cumin , toasted in a pan then crushed
- 400g can chopped tomatoes
- 2 tbsp red lentils
- 350g pack baby aubergine , quartered
- 1 reduced-salt vegetable stock cube

For the cauliflower rice

- 1 medium cauliflower
- good handful coriander , chopped
- cumin seeds , toasted (optional)

Method

STEP 1

Tip the pork into a bowl and stir in the curry powder and vinegar. Set aside. Heat the oil in a heavy-based pan and fry the onion and ginger for 10 mins, stirring frequently, until golden. Tip in the pork mixture and fry for a few mins more. Remove the pork and set aside. Stir in the toasted spices, then tip in the tomatoes, lentils and aubergine, and crumble in the stock cube. Cover and leave to simmer for 40 mins, stirring frequently, until the aubergine is almost cooked. If it starts to look dry, add a splash of water. Return the pork to the pan and cook for a further 10-20 mins until the pork is cooked and tender.

STEP 2

Just before serving, cut the hard core and stalks from the cauliflower and pulse the rest in a food processor to make grains the size of rice. Tip into a heatproof bowl, cover with cling film, then pierce and microwave for 7 mins on High – there is no need to add any water. Stir in the coriander and serve with the curry. For spicier rice, add some toasted cumin seeds.

Hake & seafood cataplana

Prep:15 mins **Cook:**35 mins

Serves 2

Ingredients

- 2 tbsp cold-pressed rapeseed oil
- 1 onion , halved and thinly sliced
- 250g salad potatoes , cut into chunks
- 1 large red pepper , deseeded and chopped
- 1 courgette (200g), thickly sliced
- 2 tomatoes , chopped (150g)
- 2 large garlic cloves , finely grated
- 1 tbsp cider vinegar (optional)
- 2 tsp vegetable bouillon powder
- 2 skinless hake fillets (pack size 240g)
- 150g pack ready-cooked mussels (not in shells)
- 60g peeled prawns
- large handful of parsley , chopped

Method

STEP 1

Heat the oil in a wide non-stick pan with a tight-fitting lid. Fry the onions and potatoes for about 5 mins, or until starting to soften. Add the peppers, courgettes, tomatoes and garlic, then stir in the vinegar, if using, the bouillon and 200ml water. Bring to a simmer, cover and cook for 25 mins, or until the peppers and courgettes are very tender (if your pan doesn't have a tight-fitting lid, wet a sheet of baking parchment and place over the stew before covering – this helps keep in the juices).

STEP 2

Add the hake fillets, mussels and prawns, then cover and cook for 5 mins more, or until the fish flakes easily when tested with a fork. Scatter over the parsley and serve.

Herb & garlic pork with summer ratatouille

Prep: 15 mins **Cook:** 25 mins

4 (or 2 with leftovers for other meals)

Ingredients

- 2 tsp rapeseed oil
- 2 red onions , halved and sliced
- 2 peppers (any colour), diced
- 1 large aubergine , diced
- 2 large courgettes , halved and sliced
- 2 garlic cloves , chopped
- 400g can chopped tomatoes
- 2 tsp vegetable bouillon
- 1 thyme spig
- handful basil , stalks chopped, leaves torn and kept separate

For the pork

- 475g pork tenderloin, fat trimmed off, cut into 2 equal pieces
- 2 garlic cloves , crushed
- 1 tbsp thyme leaves , plus a few sprigs to decorate
- 1 tsp rapeseed oil
- brown rice or new potatoes, to serve

Method

STEP 1

Heat the oil in a large non-stick pan and fry the onions for 5 mins or until softened. Stir in the peppers, aubergine, courgettes and garlic, and cook, stirring, for a few mins. Tip in the tomatoes and 1 can of water, then stir in the bouillon, thyme and basil stalks. Cover and simmer for 20 mins or until tender. Stir through the basil leaves.

STEP 2

Meanwhile, rub the pork with the garlic, then scatter with the thyme and some black pepper, patting it so it sticks all over. Heat the oil in a non-stick frying pan and cook the pork for about 12 mins, turning frequently so it browns on all sides, until tender but still moist. Cover and rest for 5 mins.

STEP 3

If you're making this as part of the Healthy Diet Plan, set aside half of the pork to use in the curried pork bulghar salad later in the week and store in the fridge once cooled. Chill the half of the ratatouille and use it to make the ratatouille pasta salad with rocket for another day. If you are serving four you can skip this step.

STEP 4

To serve, slice the pork and serve with the ratatouille, some brown rice or new potatoes and some extra thyme.

Smashed chicken with corn slaw

Prep:10 mins **Cook:**5 mins

Serves 4

Ingredients

For the chicken

- 4 skinless chicken breast fillets
- 1 lime , zested and juiced
- 2 tbsp bio yogurt
- 1 tsp fresh thyme leaves
- ¼ tsp turmeric
- 2 tbsp finely chopped coriander
- 1 garlic clove , finely grated
- 1 tsp rapeseed oil

For the slaw

- 1 small avocado
- 1 lime , zested and juiced
- 2 tbsp bio yogurt
- 2 tbsp finely chopped coriander
- 160g corn , cut from 2 cobs
- 1 red pepper , deseeded and chopped
- 1 red onion , halved and finely sliced
- 320g white cabbage , finely sliced
- 150g new potatoes , boiled, to serve

Method

STEP 1

Cut the chicken breasts in half, then put them between two sheets of baking parchment and bash with a rolling pin to flatten. Mix the lime zest and juice with the yogurt, thyme, turmeric, coriander and garlic in a large bowl. Add the chicken and stir until well coated. Leave to marinate while you make the slaw.

STEP 2

Mash the avocado with the lime juice and zest, 2 tbsp yogurt and the coriander. Stir in the corn, red pepper, onion and cabbage.

STEP 3

Heat a large non-stick frying pan or griddle pan, then cook the chicken in batches for a few mins each side – they'll cook quickly as they're thin. Serve the hot chicken with the slaw and the new potatoes. If you're cooking for two, chill half the chicken and slaw for lunch another day (eat within two days).

Soup maker tomato soup

Prep:5 mins **Cook:**30 mins

Serves 2

Ingredients

- 500g ripe tomatoes , off the vine and quartered or halved
- 1 small onion , chopped
- ½ small carrot , chopped
- ½ celery stick, chopped
- 1 tsp tomato purée
- pinch of sugar
- 450ml vegetable stock

Method

STEP 1

Put all the ingredients into the soup maker and press the 'smooth soup' function. Make sure you don't fill the soup maker above the max fill line.

STEP 2

Once the cycle is complete, season well, and check the soup for sweetness. Add a little more sugar, salt or tomato puree for depth of colour, if you like.

Leek, tomato & barley risotto with pan-cooked cod

Prep:10 mins **Cook:**20 mins

Serves 2

Ingredients

- 2 tsp rapeseed oil
- 1 large leek (315g), thinly sliced
- 2 garlic cloves , chopped
- 400g can barley (don't drain)
- 2 tsp vegetable bouillon
- 1 tsp finely chopped sage
- 1 tbsp thyme leaves , plus a few extra to serve
- 160g cherry tomatoes
- 50g finely grated parmesan
- 2 skin-on cod fillets or firm white fish fillets

Method

STEP 1

Heat 1 tsp oil in a non-stick pan and fry the leek and garlic for 5-10 mins, stirring frequently until softened, adding a splash of water to help it cook if you need to.

STEP 2

Tip in the barley with its liquid, then stir in the bouillon, sage and thyme. Simmer, stirring frequently for 3-4 mins. Add the tomatoes and cook about 4-5 mins more until they soften and start to split, adding a drop more water if necessary. Stir in the parmesan.

STEP 3

Meanwhile, heat the remaining oil in a non-stick pan and fry the cod, skin-side down, for 4-5 mins. Flip the fillets over to cook briefly on the other side. Spoon the risotto into two bowls. Serve the cod on top with a few thyme leaves, if you like.

Green minestrone with tortellini

Prep:5 mins **Cook:**25 mins

Serves 4

Ingredients

- 2 tbsp olive or rapeseed oil

- 1 onion , chopped
- 1 small leek , chopped
- 1 celery stick , chopped
- 3 garlic cloves , crushed
- 2 bay leaves
- 1l good-quality chicken or vegetable stock
- 100g shredded spring veg or cabbage
- 50g frozen peas
- 1 lemon , zested
- 250g tortellini

Method

STEP 1

Heat the olive or rapeseed oil in a large pan. Add the onion, leek and celery stick. Cook for 8-10 mins until softened, then stir in the garlic and bay leaves. Pour in the chicken or vegetable stock, then cover and simmer for 10 mins. Add the spring veg or cabbage, peas, lemon zest and tortellini (spinach tortellini works well). Cover and cook for another 3 mins, season well and ladle into bowls.

Easy vegan pho

Prep:10 mins **Cook:**20 mins

Serves 2

Ingredients

- 100g rice noodles
- 1 tsp Marmite
- 1 tsp vegetable oil
- 50g chestnut mushrooms , sliced
- 1 leek , sliced
- 2 tbsp soy sauce

To serve

- 1 red chilli , sliced (deseeded if you don't like it too hot)

- ½ bunch mint , leaves picked and stalk discarded
- handful salted peanuts
- sriracha , to serve

Method

STEP 1

Tip the noodles into a bowl and cover with boiling water. Leave to stand for 10 mins, then drain, rinse in cold water and set aside.

STEP 2

In a jug, mix the Marmite with 500ml boiling water. Set aside while you cook the vegetables.

STEP 3

Heat the oil in a saucepan, then add the mushrooms and leek. Cook for 10-15 mins until softened and beginning to colour, then add the soy sauce and Marmite and water mixture and stir. Bring to the boil for 5 mins.

STEP 4

Divide the noodles between two deep bowls, then ladle over the hot broth. Top with the chilli slices, mint leaves and peanuts, and serve with some sriracha on the side.

All-in–one chicken with wilted spinach

Prep:20 mins **Cook:**1 hr

Serves 2

Ingredients

- 2 beetroot , peeled and cut into small chunks
- 300g celeriac , cut into small chunks
- 2 red onions , quartered
- 8 garlic cloves , 4 crushed, the rest left whole, but peeled
- 1 tbsp rapeseed oil
- 1½ tbsp fresh thyme leaves , plus extra to serve
- 1 lemon , zested and juiced
- 1 tsp fennel seeds

- 1 tsp English mustard powder
- 1 tsp smoked paprika
- 4 tbsp bio yogurt
- 4 bone-in chicken thighs , skin removed
- 260g bag spinach

Method

STEP 1

Heat oven to 200C/180C fan/gas 6. Tip the beetroot, celeriac, onions and whole garlic cloves into a shallow roasting tin. Add the oil, 1 tbsp thyme, half the lemon zest, fennel seeds and a squeeze of lemon juice, then toss together. Roast for 20 mins while you prepare the chicken.

STEP 2

Stir the mustard powder and paprika into 2 tbsp yogurt in a bowl. Add half the crushed garlic, the remaining lemon zest and thyme, and juice from half the lemon. Add the chicken and toss well until it's coated all over. Put the chicken in the tin with the veg and roast for 40 mins until the chicken is cooked through and the vegetables are tender.

STEP 3

About 5 mins before the chicken is ready, wash and drain the spinach and put it in a pan with the remaining crushed garlic. Cook until wilted, then turn off the heat and stir in the remaining yogurt. Scatter some extra thyme over the chicken and vegetables, then serve.

Baked piri-piri tilapia with crushed potatoes

Prep:10 mins **Cook:**25 mins

Serves 4

Ingredients

- 600g small new potatoes
- 2 red peppers, cut into chunky pieces
- 1 tbsp red wine vinegar
- drizzle of extra virgin olive oil
- 4 large pieces tilapia or cod
- green salad, to serve

For the piri-piri sauce

- 6 hot pickled peppers (I used Peppadew)
- 1 tsp chilli flakes
- 2 garlic cloves
- juice and zest 1 lemon
- 1 tbsp red wine vinegar
- 2 tbsp extra virgin olive oil
- 1 tbsp smoked paprika

Method

STEP 1

Heat oven to 220C/200C fan/gas 7. Boil the potatoes until knife-tender, then drain. Spread out on a large baking tray and gently crush with the back of a spatula. Add the peppers, drizzle with the vinegar and oil, season well and roast for 25 mins.

STEP 2

Put the piri-piri ingredients in a food processor with some salt. Purée until fine, then pour into a bowl. Put the fish on a baking tray and spoon over some of the piri-piri sauce. Season and bake for the final 10 mins of the potatoes' cooking time. Serve everything with the extra sauce and a green salad on the side.

Seared beef salad with capers & mint

Prep:10 mins **Cook:**12 mins

Serves 2

Ingredients

- 150g new potatoes , thickly sliced
- 160g fine green beans , trimmed and halved
- 160g frozen peas
- rapeseed oil , for brushing
- 200g lean fillet steak , trimmed of any fat
- 160g romaine lettuce , roughly torn into pieces

For the dressing

- 1 tbsp extra virgin olive oil
- 2 tsp cider vinegar
- ½ tsp English mustard powder
- 2 tbsp chopped mint
- 3 tbsp chopped basil
- 1 garlic clove , finely grated
- 1 tbsp capers

Method

STEP 1

Cook the potatoes in a pan of simmering water for 5 mins. Add the beans and cook 5 mins more, then tip in the peas and cook for 2 mins until all the vegetables are just tender. Drain.

STEP 2

Meanwhile, measure all the dressing ingredients in a large bowl and season with black pepper. Stir and crush the herbs and capers with the back of a spoon to intensify their flavours.

STEP 3

Brush a little oil over the steak and grind over some black pepper. Heat a non-stick frying pan over a high heat and cook the steak for 4 mins on one side and 2-3 mins on the other, depending on the thickness and how rare you like it. Transfer to a plate to rest while you carry on with the rest of the salad.

STEP 4

Mix the warm vegetables into the dressing until well coated, then add the lettuce and toss again. Pile onto plates. Slice the steak and turn in any dressing left in the bowl, add to the salad and serve while still warm.

Minty griddled chicken & peach salad

Prep:10 mins **Cook:**15 mins

Serves 2

Ingredients

- 1 lime , zested and juiced
- 1 tbsp rapeseed oil
- 2 tbsp mint , finely chopped, plus a few leaves to serve
- 1 garlic clove , finely grated
- 2 skinless chicken breast fillets (300g)
- 160g fine beans , trimmed and halved
- 2 peaches (200g), each cut into 8 thick wedges
- 1 red onion , cut into wedges
- 1 large Little Gem lettuce (165g), roughly shredded
- ½ x 60g pack rocket
- 1 small avocado , stoned and sliced
- 240g cooked new potatoes

Method

STEP 1

Mix the lime zest and juice, oil and mint, then put half in a bowl with the garlic. Thickly slice the chicken at a slight angle, add to the garlic mixture and toss together with plenty of black pepper.

STEP 2

Cook the beans in a pan of water for 3-4 mins until just tender. Meanwhile, griddle the chicken and onion for a few mins each side until cooked and tender. Transfer to a plate, then quickly griddle the peaches. If you don't have a griddle pan, use a non-stick frying pan with a drop of oil.

STEP 3

Toss the warm beans and onion in the remaining mint mixture, and pile onto a platter or into individual shallow bowls with the lettuce and rocket. Top with the avocado, peaches and chicken and scatter over the mint. Serve with the potatoes while still warm.

Parma pork with potato salad

Prep:15 mins **Cook:**15 mins

Serves 2

Ingredients

- 175g new potatoes (we used Jersey Royals), scrubbed and thickly sliced
- 3 celery sticks, thickly sliced
- 3 tbsp bio yogurt
- 2 gherkins (about 85g each), sliced
- ¼ tsp caraway seeds
- ½ tsp Dijon mustard
- 2 x 100g pieces lean pork tenderloin
- 2 tsp chopped sage
- 2 slices Parma ham
- 1 tsp rapeseed oil
- 2 tsp balsamic vinegar
- 2 handfuls salad leaves

Method

STEP 1

Bring a pan of water to the boil, add the potatoes and celery and cook for 8 mins. Meanwhile, mix the yogurt, guerkins, caraway and mustard in a bowl. When the potatoes and celery are cooked, drain and set aside for a few mins to cool a little.

STEP 2

Bash the pork pieces with a rolling pin to flatten them. Sprinkle over the sage and some pepper, then top each with a slice of Parma ham. Heat the oil in a non-stick pan, add the pork and cook for a couple of mins each side, turning carefully. Add the balsamic vinegar and let it sizzle in the pan.

STEP 3

Stir the potatoes and celery into the dressing and serve with the pork, with some salad leaves on the side.

Yaki udon

Prep: 10 mins **Cook:** 5 mins

Serves 2

Ingredients

- 250g dried udon noodles (400g frozen or fresh)
- 2 tbsp sesame oil
- 1 onion, thickly sliced
- ¼ head white cabbage, roughly sliced
- 10 shiitake mushrooms
- 4 spring onions, finely sliced

For the sauce

- 4 tbsp mirin
- 2 tbsp soy sauce
- 1 tbsp caster sugar
- 1 tbsp Worcestershire sauce (or vegetarian alternative)

Method

STEP 1

Boil some water in a large saucepan. Add 250ml cold water and the udon noodles. (As they are so thick, adding cold water helps them to cook a little bit slower so the middle cooks through). If using frozen or fresh noodles, cook for 2 mins or until al dente; dried will take longer, about 5-6 mins. Drain and leave in the colander.

STEP 2

Heat 1 tbsp of the oil, add the onion and cabbage and sauté for 5 mins until softened. Add the mushrooms and some spring onions, and sauté for 1 more min. Pour in the remaining sesame oil and the noodles. If using cold noodles, let them heat through before adding the ingredients for the sauce – otherwise tip in straight away and keep stir-frying until sticky and piping hot. Sprinkle with the remaining spring onions.

Mushroom & potato soup

Prep:15 mins **Cook:**30 mins

Serves 4

Ingredients

- 1 tbsp rapeseed oil
- 2 large onions , halved and thinly sliced
- 20g dried porcini mushrooms
- 3 tsp vegetable bouillon powder
- 300g chestnut mushrooms , chopped
- 3 garlic cloves , finely grated
- 300g potato , finely diced
- 2 tsp fresh thyme
- 4 carrots , finely diced
- 2 tbsp chopped parsley
- 8 tbsp bio yogurt
- 55g walnut pieces

Method

STEP 1

Heat the oil in a large pan. Tip in the onions and fry for 10 mins until golden. Meanwhile, pour 1.2 litres boiling water over the dried mushrooms and stir in the bouillon.

STEP 2

Add the fresh mushrooms and garlic to the pan with the potatoes, thyme and carrots, and continue to fry until the mushrooms soften and start to brown.

STEP 3

Pour in the dried mushrooms and stock, cover the pan and leave to simmer for 20 mins. Stir in the parsley and plenty of pepper. Ladle into bowls and serve each portion topped with 2 tbsp yogurt and a quarter of the walnuts. The rest can be chilled and reheated the next day.

Low-fat cherry cheesecake

Prep:1 hr **Cook:**30 mins Plus overnight chilling

Cuts into 8 slices

Ingredients

- 25g butter , melted
- 140g amaretti biscuit , crushed

- 3 sheets leaf gelatine
- zest and juice 1 orange
- 2 x 250g tubs quark
- 250g tub ricotta
- 2 tsp vanilla extract
- 100g icing sugar

For the topping

- 400g fresh cherry , stoned
- 5 tbsp cherry jam
- 1 tbsp cornflour

Method

STEP 1

Line the sides of a 20cm round loose-bottomed cake tin with baking parchment. Stir the butter into twothirds of the biscuit crumbs, and reserve the rest. Sprinkle the buttery crumbs over the base of the tin and press down. Soak the gelatine in cold water for 5-10 mins until soft.

STEP 2

Warm the orange juice in a small pan or the microwave until almost boiling. Squeeze the gelatine of excess water, then stir into the juice to dissolve.

STEP 3

Beat the quark, ricotta, vanilla and icing sugar together with an electric whisk until really smooth. Then, with the beaters still running, pour in the juice mixture and beat to combine. Pour the cheesecake mixture over the crumbs and smooth the top. Cover with cling film and chill overnight.

STEP 4

To make the topping, put the cherries in a pan with the orange zest and 100ml water. Cook, covered, for 15 mins until the cherries are softened. Put one-third of the cherries in a bowl and mash with a potato masher to give you a chunky compote. Return to the pan, add the jam, cornflour and 2 tbsp water, and mix to combine. Cook until thickened and saucy – if the sauce is too dry, add a splash more water. Cool to room temperature.

STEP 5

Just before serving, carefully remove the cheesecake from the tin and peel off the parchment. Scatter over the remaining biscuit crumbs and some cherry sauce. Serve in slices with the remaining cherry sauce alongside.

Veggie okonomiyaki

Prep:15 mins **Cook:**10 mins

Serves 2

Ingredients

- 3 large eggs
- 50g plain flour
- 50ml milk
- 4 spring onions , trimmed and sliced
- 1 pak choi , sliced
- 200g Savoy cabbage , shredded
- 1 red chilli , deseeded and finely chopped, plus extra to serve
- ½ tbsp low-salt soy sauce
- ½ tbsp rapeseed oil
- 1 heaped tbsp low-fat mayonnaise
- ½ lime , juiced
- sushi ginger , to serve (optional)
- wasabi , to serve (optional)

Method

STEP 1

Whisk together the eggs, flour and milk until smooth. Add half the spring onions, the pak choi, cabbage, chilli and soy sauce. Heat the oil in a small frying pan and pour in the batter. Cook, covered, over a medium heat for 7-8 mins. Flip the okonomiyaki into a second frying pan, then return it to the heat and cook for a further 7-8 mins until a skewer inserted into it comes out clean.

STEP 2

Mix the mayonnaise and lime juice together in a small bowl. Transfer the okonomiyaki to a plate, then drizzle over the lime mayo and top with the extra chilli and spring onion and the sushi ginger, if using. Serve with the wasabi on the side, if you like.

Easy chicken stew

Prep:10 mins **Cook:**50 mins

Serves 4

Ingredients

- 1 tbsp olive oil
- 1 bunch spring onions , sliced, white and green parts separated
- 1 small swede (350g), peeled and chopped into small pieces
- 400g potatoes , peeled and chopped into small pieces
- 8 skinless boneless chicken thighs
- 1 tbsp Dijon mustard
- 500ml chicken stock
- 200g Savoy cabbage or spring cabbage, sliced
- 2 tsp cornflour (optional)
- crusty bread or cheese scones, to serve (optional)

Method

STEP 1

Heat the oil in a large saucepan. Add the white spring onion slices and fry for 1 min to soften. Tip in the swede and potatoes and cook for 2-3 mins more, then add the chicken, mustard and stock. Cover and cook for 35 mins, or until the vegetables are tender and the chicken cooked through.

STEP 2

Add the cabbage and simmer for another 5 mins. If the stew looks too thin, mix the cornflour with 1 tbsp cold water and pour a couple of teaspoonfuls into the pan; let the stew bubble and thicken, then check again. If it's still too thin, add a little more of the cornflour mix and let the stew bubble and thicken some more.

STEP 3

Season to taste, then spoon the stew into deep bowls. Scatter over the green spring onion slices and serve with crusty bread or warm cheese scones, if you like.

Green chowder with prawns

Prep: 10 mins **Cook:** 20 mins - 30 mins

Serves 4

Ingredients

- 1 tbsp olive oil
- 1 onion , finely chopped
- 1 celery stick , finely chopped
- 1 garlic clove
- 300g petit pois
- 200g pack sliced kale
- 2 potatoes , finely chopped
- 1 low-salt chicken stock cube (we used Kallo)
- 100g cooked North Atlantic prawns

Method

STEP 1

Heat the oil in a saucepan over a medium heat. Add the onion and celery and cook for 5-6 mins until softened but not coloured. Add the garlic and cook for a further min. Stir in the petit pois, kale and potatoes, then add the stock cube and 750ml water. Bring to the boil and simmer for 10-12 mins until the potatoes are soft.

STEP 2

Tip ¾ of the mixture into a food processor and whizz until smooth. Add a little more water or stock if it's too thick. Pour the mixture back into the pan and add half the prawns.

STEP 3

Divide between four bowls and spoon the remaining prawns on top. Can be frozen for up to a month. Add the prawns once defrosted.

Mushroom brunch

Prep: 5 mins **Cook:** 12 mins - 15 mins

Serves 4

Ingredients

- 250g mushrooms
- 1 garlic clove
- 1 tbsp olive oil
- 160g bag kale
- 4 eggs

Method

STEP 1

Slice the mushrooms and crush the garlic clove. Heat the olive oil in a large non-stick frying pan, then fry the garlic over a low heat for 1 min. Add the mushrooms and cook until soft. Then, add the kale. If the kale won't all fit in the pan, add half and stir until wilted, then add the rest. Once all the kale is wilted, season.

STEP 2

Now crack in the eggs and keep them cooking gently for 2-3 mins. Then, cover with the lid to for a further 2-3 mins or until the eggs are cooked to your liking. Serve with bread.

Thai fried prawn & pineapple rice

Prep: 10 mins **Cook:** 15 mins

Serves 4

Ingredients

- 2 tsp sunflower oil
- bunch spring onions , greens and whites separated, both sliced
- 1 green pepper , deseeded and chopped into small chunks
- 140g pineapple , chopped into bite-sized chunks
- 3 tbsp Thai green curry paste

- 4 tsp light soy sauce , plus extra to serve
- 300g cooked basmati rice (brown, white or a mix - about 140g uncooked rice)
- 2 large eggs , beaten
- 140g frozen peas
- 225g can bamboo shoots , drained
- 250g frozen prawns , cooked or raw
- 2-3 limes , 1 juiced, the rest cut into wedges to serve
- handful coriander leaves (optional)

Method

STEP 1

Heat the oil in a wok or non-stick frying pan and fry the spring onion whites for 2 mins until softened. Stir in the pepper for 1 min, followed by the pineapple for 1 min more, then stir in the green curry paste and soy sauce.

STEP 2

Add the rice, stir-frying until piping hot, then push the rice to one side of the pan and scramble the eggs on the other side. Stir the peas, bamboo shoots and prawns into the rice and eggs, then heat through for 2 mins until the prawns are hot and the peas tender. Finally, stir in the spring onion greens, lime juice and coriander, if using. Spoon into bowls and serve with extra lime wedges and soy sauce.

Feta & clementine lunch bowl

Prep:15 mins **Cook:**15 mins

Serves 2

Ingredients

- 1 red onion , halved and thinly sliced
- 1 lemon , zested and juiced
- 2 clementines , 1 zested, flesh sliced
- 2 garlic cloves , chopped
- 400g can green lentils , drained
- 1 tbsp balsamic vinegar
- 1 ½ tbsp rapeseed oil

- 1 red pepper , quartered and sliced
- 60g feta , crumbled
- small handful mint , chopped
- 4 walnut halves , chopped

Method

STEP 1

Mix the onion with the lemon juice, lemon and clementine zest and garlic.

STEP 2

Tip the lentils into two bowls or lunchboxes and drizzle over the balsamic and 1 tbsp oil. Heat the remaining oil in a large non-stick wok, add the pepper and stir-fry for 3 mins. Tip in half the onion and cook until tender. Pile on top of the lentils, then mix the clementines, remaining onions, feta, mint and walnut pieces.

Carrot & ginger soup

Prep:15 mins **Cook:**25 mins - 30 mins

Serves 4

Ingredients

- 1 tbsp rapeseed oil
- 1 large onion, chopped
- 2 tbsp coarsely grated ginger
- 2 garlic cloves, sliced
- ½ tsp ground nutmeg
- 850ml vegetable stock
- 500g carrot (preferably organic), sliced
- 400g can cannellini beans (no need to drain)

Supercharged topping

- 4 tbsp almonds in their skins, cut into slivers
- sprinkle of nutmeg

Method

STEP 1

Heat the oil in a large pan, add the onion, ginger and garlic, and fry for 5 mins until starting to soften. Stir in the nutmeg and cook for 1 min more.

STEP 2

Pour in the stock, add the carrots, beans and their liquid, then cover and simmer for 20-25 mins until the carrots are tender.

STEP 3

Scoop a third of the mixture into a bowl and blitz the remainder with a hand blender or in a food processor until smooth. Return everything to the pan and heat until bubbling. Serve topped with the almonds and nutmeg.

Sausage & butternut squash shells

Prep:15 mins **Cook:**35 mins

Serves 4

Ingredients

- 1 medium butternut squash , peeled and cut into medium chunks
- 1 ½ tbsp olive oil
- 2 garlic cloves , crushed
- 1 fennel bulb , thinly sliced (keep the green fronds to serve)
- 4 spring onions , thinly sliced
- 2 tsp chilli flakes
- 1 tsp fennel seeds
- 300g large pasta shells
- 3 pork sausages

Method

STEP 1

Put the squash in a microwaveable bowl with a splash of water. Cover with cling film and cook on high for 10 mins until soft. Tip into a blender.

STEP 2

Meanwhile, put a frying pan over a medium heat and pour in 1 tbsp olive oil. Add the garlic, sliced fennel, spring onions, half the chilli flakes, half the fennel seeds and a splash of water. Cook, stirring occasionally, for 5 mins until softened. Scrape into the blender with squash. Blitz to a smooth sauce, adding enough water to get to a creamy consistency. Season to taste.

STEP 3

Bring a pan of water to the boil and cook the pasta for 1 min less than the pack instructions. Put the frying pan back on the heat (don't bother washing it first – it's all flavour). Pour in the remaining oil, squeeze the sausagemeat from the skins into the pan and add the remaining chilli and remaining fennel seeds. Fry until browned and crisp, breaking down the sausagemeat with a spoon.

STEP 4

Drain the pasta and return to its pan on the heat. Pour in the butternut sauce and give everything a good mix to warm the sauce through. Divide between bowls and top with the crispy sausage mix and fennel fronds.

Miso mushroom & tofu noodle soup

Prep: 10 mins **Cook:** 15 mins

Serves 1

Ingredients

- 1 tbsp rapeseed oil
- 70g mixed mushrooms , sliced
- 50g smoked tofu , cut into small cubes
- ½ tbsp brown rice miso paste
- 50g dried buckwheat or egg noodles
- 2 spring onions , shredded

Method

STEP 1

Heat half the oil in a frying pan over a medium heat. Add the mushrooms and fry for 5-6 mins, or until golden. Transfer to a bowl using a slotted spoon and set aside. Add the remaining oil to the pan and fry the tofu for 3-4 mins, or until evenly golden.

STEP 2

Mix the miso paste with 325ml boiling water in a jug. Cook the noodles following pack instructions, then drain and transfer to a bowl. Top with the mushrooms and tofu, then pour over the miso broth. Scatter over the spring onions just before serving.

Mexican egg roll

Prep:5 mins **Cook:**10 mins

Serves 2

Ingredients

- 1 large egg
- a little rapeseed oil for frying
- 2 tbsp tomato salsa
- about 1 tbsp fresh coriander

Method

STEP 1

Beat the egg with 1 tbsp water. Heat the oil in a medium non-stick pan. Add the egg and swirl round the base of the pan, as though you are making a pancake, and cook until set. There is no need to turn it.

STEP 2

Carefully tip the pancake onto a board, spread with the salsa, sprinkle with the coriander, then roll it up. It can be eaten warm or cold – you can keep it for 2 days in the fridge.

Miso aubergines

Prep:5 mins **Cook:**50 mins

Serves 2

Ingredients

- 2 small aubergines, halved
- vegetable oil, for roasting and frying

- 50g brown miso
- 100g giant couscous
- 1 red chilli, thinly sliced
- ½ small pack coriander, leaves chopped

Method

STEP 1

Heat oven to 180C/160C fan/ gas 4. With a sharp knife, criss-cross the flesh of the aubergines in a diagonal pattern, then place on a baking tray. Brush the flesh with 1 tbsp vegetable oil.

STEP 2

Mix the miso with 25ml water to make a thick paste. Spread the paste over the aubergines, then cover the tray with foil and roast in the centre of the oven for 30 mins.

STEP 3

Remove the foil and roast the aubergines for a further 15-20 mins, depending on their size, until tender.

STEP 4

Meanwhile, bring a saucepan of salted water to the boil and heat 1 /2 tbsp vegetable oil over a medium-high heat in a frying pan. Add the couscous to the frying pan, toast for 2 mins until golden brown, then tip into the pan of boiling water and cook for 8-10 mins until tender (or following pack instructions). Drain well. Serve the aubergines with the couscous, topped with the chilli and a scattering of coriander leaves.

Sesame salmon, purple sprouting broccoli & sweet potato mash

Prep:10 mins **Cook:**15 mins

Serves 2

Ingredients

- 1 ½ tbsp sesame oil
- 1 tbsp low-salt soy sauce

- thumb-sized piece ginger, grated
- 1 garlic clove, crushed
- 1 tsp honey
- 2 sweet potatoes, scrubbed and cut into wedges
- 1 lime, cut into wedges
- 2 boneless skinless salmon fillets
- 250g purple sprouting broccoli
- 1 tbsp sesame seeds
- 1 red chilli, thinly sliced (deseeded if you don't like it too hot)

Method

STEP 1

Heat oven to 200C/180 fan/ gas 6 and line a baking tray with parchment. Mix together 1/2 tbsp sesame oil, the soy, ginger, garlic and honey. Put the sweet potato wedges, skin and all, into a glass bowl with the lime wedges. Cover with cling film and microwave on high for 12-14 mins until completely soft.

STEP 2

Meanwhile, spread the broccoli and salmon out on the baking tray. Spoon over the marinade and season. Roast in the oven for 10-12 mins, then sprinkle over the sesame seeds.

STEP 3

Remove the lime wedges and roughly mash the sweet potato using a fork. Mix in the remaining sesame oil, the chilli and some seasoning. Divide between plates, along with the salmon and broccoli.

Lighter chicken cacciatore

Prep:15 mins **Cook:**50 mins

Serves 4

Ingredients

- 1 tbsp olive oil
- 3 slices prosciutto, fat removed, chopped
- 1 medium onion, chopped

- 2 garlic cloves, finely chopped
- 2 sage sprigs
- 2 rosemary sprigs
- 4 skinless chicken breasts (550g total weight), preferably organic
- 150ml dry white wine
- 400g can plum tomatoes in natural juice
- 1 tbsp tomato purée
- 225g chestnut mushrooms, quartered or halved if large
- small handful chopped flat-leaf parsley, to serve

Method

STEP 1

Heat the oil in a large non-stick frying pan. Tip in the prosciutto and fry for about 2 mins until crisp. Remove with a slotted spoon, letting any fat drain back into the pan, and set aside. Put the onion, garlic and herbs in the pan and fry for 3-4 mins.

STEP 2

Spread the onion out in the pan, then lay the chicken breasts on top. Season with pepper and fry for 5 mins over a medium heat, turning the chicken once, until starting to brown on both sides and the onion is caramelising on the bottom of the pan. Remove the chicken and set aside on a plate. Raise the heat, give it a quick stir and, when sizzling, pour in the wine and let it bubble for 2 mins to reduce slightly.

STEP 3

Lower the heat to medium, return the prosciutto to the pan, then stir in the tomatoes (breaking them up with your spoon), tomato purée and mushrooms. Spoon 4 tbsp of water into the empty tomato can, swirl it around, then pour it into the pan. Cover and simmer for 15-20 mins or until the sauce has thickened and reduced slightly, then return the chicken to the pan and cook, uncovered, for about 15 mins or until the chicken is cooked through. Season and scatter over the parsley to serve.

Balsamic beef with beetroot & rocket

Prep:15 mins **Cook:**25 mins

Serves 2

Ingredients

- 240g beef sirloin , fat trimmed
- 1 tbsp balsamic vinegar
- 2 tsp thyme leaves
- 2 garlic cloves , 1 finely grated, 1 sliced
- 2 tsp rapeseed oil
- 2 red onions , halved and sliced
- 175g fine beans , trimmed
- 2 cooked beetroot , halved and cut into wedges
- 6 pitted Kalamata olives , quartered
- 2 handfuls rocket

Method

STEP 1

Beat the steak with a rolling pin until it is about the thickness of two £1 coins, then cut into two equal pieces. In a bowl, mix the balsamic, thyme, grated garlic, half the oil and a grinding of black pepper. Place the steaks in the marinade and set aside.

STEP 2

Heat the remaining 1 tsp oil in a large non-stick frying pan, and fry the onions and garlic for 8-10 mins, stirring frequently, until soft and starting to brown. Meanwhile, steam the beans for 4-6 mins or until just tender.

STEP 3

Push the onion mixture to one side in the pan. Lift the steaks from the bowl, shake off any excess marinade, and sear in the pan for 2½-3 mins, turning once, until cooked but still a little pink inside. Pile the beans onto plates and place the steaks on top. Add the beetroot wedges, olives and remaining marinade to the pan and cook briefly to heat through, then spoon on top and around the steaks. Add the rocket and serve.

Charred spring onions & teriyaki tofu

Prep:5 mins **Cook:**25 mins

Serves 2

Ingredients

- 150g wholegrain rice
- 50ml soy sauce
- 2 tbsp mirin
- ½ tsp grated ginger
- 1 tsp honey
- 350g firm tofu (we used Cauldron)
- 1 bunch spring onions , ends trimmed
- 2 tsp sunflower oil
- ½ tsp sesame seeds
- 1 red chilli , sliced (optional)

Method

STEP 1

Cook the rice according to pack instructions. Pour the soy sauce, mirin, ginger and honey into a small saucepan and add 50ml water. Bring to a simmer and cook for around 5 mins or until slightly thickened. Remove from the heat and set aside until needed.

STEP 2

If your tofu doesn't feel very firm, you'll need to press it. To do this, wrap the block of tofu in a few layers of kitchen paper, then weigh it down with a heavy pan or tray for 10-15 mins – the longer you press it, the firmer it will be. Cut the tofu into thick slices.

STEP 3

Heat a griddle pan over high heat and lightly brush the tofu and spring onions with the oil. Griddle the tofu and spring onion until deep char lines appear on both sides (around 4 mins each side) – you may have to do this in batches depending on the size of your griddle pan.

STEP 4

Divide the cooked rice between two plates, top with the tofu and spring onion, then drizzle with the teriyaki sauce. Garnish with the sesame seeds and sliced red chilli, if using.

Sesame chicken & prawn skewers

Prep:15 mins **Cook:**5 mins Plus marinating

Makes 20

Ingredients

- thumb-sized piece ginger , grated
- 1 large garlic clove , grated
- 1 tsp honey
- 1½ tsp soy sauce
- 1 tsp sesame oil
- ½ lime , juiced
- 1 tbsp sesame seeds
- 1 skinless chicken breast , cut into 10 pieces
- 10 raw king prawns
- 1 broccoli head , cut into 20 florets
- 20 cocktail skewers

Method

STEP 1

Combine the ginger, garlic, honey, soy sauce, sesame oil, lime juice and sesame seeds. Divide between two bowls, then add the chicken pieces to one and the prawns to the other. Toss both mixtures well, then leave to marinate in the fridge for 15 mins.

STEP 2

Cook the chicken in a frying pan over a medium-high heat for 3 mins, then push to one side and add the prawns to the other side of the pan. Cook for 2 mins until the prawns are pink and the chicken is cooked through (use two separate pans if anyone you're cooking for has an allergy or is a pescatarian). Put the broccoli in a microwaveable bowl with a splash of water, then cover and cook on high for 5 mins.

STEP 3

Thread half of the skewers with chicken and broccoli and the other half with prawns and broccoli.

Chipotle chicken tacos with pineapple salsa

Prep:10 mins **Cook:**10 mins

Serves 4

Ingredients

- 500g skinless boneless chicken thighs
- 1 tbsp vegetable oil
- 1 medium onion , chopped
- 2 tsp sweet smoked paprika
- 2 tsp ground cumin
- 2 tbsp cider vinegar
- 1 tbsp chipotle paste
- 200ml passata
- 2 tbsp soft brown sugar
- ½ small pineapple , cored, peeled and chopped
- ½ small pack coriander , chopped
- corn or flour tortillas
- hot sauce (I like Tabasco Chipotle), to serve

Method

STEP 1

In a food processor, roughly blitz the chicken thighs into chunky mince. Alternatively, chop into bite-sized pieces.

STEP 2

Heat the oil in a large saucepan. Add half the onion and the chicken mince. Season well and cook for about 5 mins on a high heat to brown, breaking up the meat with a spoon. Add the spices, vinegar, chipotle paste, passata and sugar. Cook for another 5 mins, then remove from the heat.

STEP 3

In a small bowl, mix the remaining onion, the pineapple and coriander. Serve the chicken and the pineapple salsa with warm tortillas and hot sauce.

Cod puttanesca with spinach & spaghetti

Prep:10 mins **Cook:**17 mins

Serves 2

Ingredients

- 100g wholemeal spaghetti
- 1 large onion , sliced
- 1 tbsp rapeseed oil
- 1 red chilli , deseeded and sliced
- 2 garlic cloves , chopped
- 200g cherry tomatoes , halved
- 1 tsp cider vinegar
- 2 tsp capers
- 5 Kalamata olives , halved
- ½ tsp smoked paprika
- 2 skinless cod fillet or loins
- 160g spinach leaves
- small handful chopped parsley , to serve

Method

STEP 1

Boil the spaghetti for 10 mins until al dente, adding the spinach for the last 2 mins. Meanwhile, fry the onion in the oil in a large non-stick frying pan with a lid until tender and turning golden. Stir in the chilli and garlic, then add the tomatoes.

STEP 2

Add the vinegar, capers, olives and paprika with a ladleful of the pasta water. Put the cod fillets on top, then cover the pan and cook for 5-7 mins until the fish just flakes. Drain the pasta and wilted spinach and pile on to plates, then top with the fish and sauce. Sprinkle over some parsley to serve.

Chicken & pearl barley risotto

Prep:5 mins **Cook:**40 mins

Serves 2

Ingredients

- 1 tsp sunflower oil
- 2 chicken thighs , skinless, bone in
- 2 carrots , chopped
- 2 celery sticks , chopped
- 1 onion , chopped
- 1 garlic clove , crushed
- 140g pearl barley

For the green dressing

- ½ x 60g bag fresh rocket leaves
- small handful mint , leaves only
- small handful flat-leaf parsley
- juice 1 lemon
- 1 tsp capers

Method

STEP 1

Heat a large saucepan over a medium-high heat and add the oil. Add the chicken and fry for 5 mins or until well-browned on all sides. Tip in the vegetables and cook for a further 5 mins until starting to soften. Add the garlic and pearl barley, then pour over 500ml water. Cover and leave to simmer for 25-30 mins, stirring occasionally.

STEP 2

Meanwhile, put all the dressing ingredients in the small bowl of a food processor and blitz until very finely chopped. Transfer to a bowl and set aside until serving.

STEP 3

When the pearl barley is soft, but still with a little bite, and most of the liquid has been absorbed, it's ready to serve. Season to taste and divide the risotto between two plates, adding spoonfuls of the dressing, to serve.

Hearty pasta soup

Prep:5 mins **Cook:**25 mins

Serves 4

Ingredients

- 1 tbsp olive oil
- 2 carrots, chopped
- 1 large onion, finely chopped
- 1l vegetable stock
- 400g can chopped tomato
- 200g frozen mixed peas and beans
- 250g pack fresh filled tortellini (we used spinach and ricotta)
- handful of basil leaves (optional)
- grated parmesan (or vegetarian alternative), to serve

Method

STEP 1

Heat oil in a pan. Fry the carrots and onion for 5 mins until starting to soften. Add the stock and tomatoes, then simmer for 10 mins. Add the peas and beans with 5 mins to go.

STEP 2

Once veg is tender, stir in the pasta. Return to the boil and simmer for 2 mins until the pasta is just cooked. Stir in the basil, if using. Season, then serve in bowls topped with a sprinkling of Parmesan and slices of garlic bread.

Spinach & barley risotto

Prep:10 mins **Cook:**15 mins

Serves 2

Ingredients

- 2 tsp rapeseed oil
- 1 large leek (315g), thinly sliced

- 2 garlic cloves , chopped
- 2 x 400g can barley , undrained
- 1 tbsp vegetable bouillon powder
- 1 tsp finely chopped sage
- 1 tbsp thyme leaves
- 160g cherry tomatoes , halved
- 160g spinach
- 50g finely grated vegetarian Italian-style hard cheese

Method

STEP 1

Heat the oil in a non-stick pan and fry the leek and garlic for 5-10 mins, stirring frequently, until softened, adding a splash of water if it sticks.

STEP 2

Tip in the cans of barley and their liquid, then stir in the bouillon powder, sage and thyme. Simmer, stirring frequently, for 4-5 mins. Add the tomatoes and spinach and cook for 2-3 mins more until the spinach is wilted, adding a splash more water if needed. Stir in most of the cheese, then serve with the remaining cheese scattered over.

Herb & garlic baked cod with romesco sauce & spinach

Prep:10 mins **Cook:**20 mins

Serves 2

Ingredients

- 2 x 140g skinless cod loin or pollock fillets
- 1 tbsp rapeseed oil, plus 2 tsp
- 1 tsp fresh thyme leaves
- 1 large garlic clove, finely grated
- ½ lemon, zested and juiced
- 1 large red pepper, sliced
- 2 leeks, well washed and thinly sliced

- 2 tbsp flaked almonds
- 1 tbsp tomato purée
- ¼ tsp vegetable bouillon powder
- 1 tsp apple cider vinegar
- 100g baby spinach, wilted in a pan or the microwave

Method

STEP 1

Heat oven to 220C/200C fan/ gas 7 and put the fish fillets in a shallow ovenproof dish so they fit quite snugly in a single layer. Mix 1 tbsp rapeseed oil with the thyme and garlic, spoon over the fish, then grate over the lemon zest. Bake for 10-12 mins until the fish is moist and flakes easily when tested.

STEP 2

Meanwhile, heat the remaining oil in a non-stick pan and fry the pepper and leeks for 5 mins until softened. Add the almonds and cook for 5 mins more. Tip in the tomato purée, 5 tbsp water, the bouillion powder and vinegar, and cook briefly to warm the mixture through.

STEP 3

Add the juice of up to half a lemon and blitz with a stick blender until it makes a thick, pesto-like sauce. Serve with the fish and the wilted spinach.

Peri-peri chicken pilaf

Prep:20 mins **Cook:**40 mins

Serves 4

Ingredients

- 1 tbsp olive oil
- pack of 6 skinless boneless chicken thighs , cut into large chunks
- 2 tbsp peri-peri seasoning
- 1 onion , finely chopped
- 2 garlic cloves , crushed
- 350g basmati rice
- 500ml hot chicken stock

- 3 peppers (any colour you like), sliced into strips
- 3 large tomatoes , deseeded and roughly chopped
- small pack parsley , roughly chopped
- 2 red chillies , sliced (optional)
- ½ lemon , cut into wedges, to serve

Method

STEP 1

Heat the oil in a large pan over a medium heat. Rub the chicken with 1 tbsp of the peri-peri and brown in the pan for 1 min each side until golden. Transfer to a plate and set aside.

STEP 2

Add the onion to the pan and cook on a gentle heat for 8-10 mins until soft. Add the garlic and remaining peri-peri, and give everything a stir. Tip in the rice and stir to coat.

STEP 3

Add the stock and return the chicken to the pan. Add the peppers and cover with a lid, then simmer gently for 25 mins until cooked. About 5 mins before the end of cooking, add the tomatoes.

STEP 4

Stir through the parsley, scatter over the chillies (if you like it spicy) and serve with lemon wedges.

Pepper & lemon spaghetti with basil & pine nuts

Prep:7 mins **Cook:**25 mins

Serves 2

Ingredients

- 1 tbsp rapeseed oil
- 1 red pepper , deseeded and diced
- 150g wholemeal spaghetti
- 2 courgettes (250g), grated
- 2 garlic cloves , finely grated

- 1 lemon , zested and juiced
- 15g basil , finely chopped
- 25g pine nuts , toasted
- 2 tbsp finely grated parmesan or vegetarian alternative (optional)

Method

STEP 1

Heat the oil in a large non-stick frying pan. Add the pepper and cook for 5 mins. Meanwhile, cook the pasta for 10-12 mins until tender.

STEP 2

Add the courgette and garlic to the pepper and cook, stirring very frequently, for 10-15 mins until the courgette is really soft.

STEP 3

Stir in the lemon zest and juice, basil and spaghetti (reserve some pasta water) and toss together, adding a little of the pasta water until nicely coated. Add the pine nuts, then spoon into bowls and serve topped with the parmesan, if using.

Chicken & sweetcorn soup

Prep:10 mins **Cook:**2 hrs and 15 mins

Serves 2

Ingredients

- 1 chicken carcass
- 4 thin slices fresh ginger, plus 1 tbsp finely grated
- 2 onions, quartered
- 3 garlic cloves, finely grated
- 2 tsp apple cider vinegar
- 325g can sweetcorn
- 3 spring onions, whites thinly sliced, greens sliced at an angle
- 100g cooked chicken, shredded
- 2 tsp tamari
- 2 eggs, beaten

- few drops sesame oil, to serve (optional)

Method

STEP 1

Boil a large kettle of water. Break the carcass into a big non-stick pan and add the ginger slices, onion and two-thirds of the garlic. Cook, stirring, for about 2 mins – the meat will stick to the base of the pan, but this will add to the flavour. Pour in 1.5 litres of boiling water, stir in the vinegar, then cover and simmer for 2 hrs.

STEP 2

Put a large sieve over a bowl and pour through the contents of the pan. Measure the liquid in the bowl – you want around 450ml. If you have too much, return to the pan and boil with the lid off to reduce it. Transfer the onion from the sieve to a bowl with three-quarters of the sweetcorn. Blitz until smooth with a hand blender.

STEP 3

Return the broth to the pan, and tip in the puréed corn, remaining sweetcorn and garlic, the grated ginger, the whites of the spring onions and the chicken. Simmer for 5 mins, then stir in the tamari. Turn off the heat, and quickly drizzle in the egg, stirring a little to create egg threads. Season with pepper, then ladle into the bowls. Top with the spring onion greens and a few drops of sesame oil, if using.

Chocolate chia pudding

Prep: 5 mins No cook, plus 4 hours chilling

Serves 4

Ingredients

- 60g chia seeds
- 400ml unsweetened almond milk or hazelnut milk
- 3 tbsp cacao powder
- 2 tbsp maple syrup
- ½ tsp vanilla extract
- cacao nibs , mixed
- frozen berries , to serve

Method

STEP 1

Put all the ingredients in a large bowl with a generous pinch of sea salt and whisk to combine. Cover with cling film then leave to thicken in the fridge for at least 4 hours, or overnight.

STEP 2

Spoon the pudding into four glasses, then top with the frozen berries and cacao nibs.

Lime prawn cocktail pitta salad

Prep:10 mins **Cook:**15 mins

Serves 2

Ingredients

- ½ wholemeal pitta
- ½ tbsp rapeseed oil
- 1 tsp Tabasco
- 1 tsp low-sugar, low-salt ketchup
- 1 tbsp low-fat mayonnaise
- 1 tbsp fat-free natural yogurt
- ½ lime , zested and juiced, plus wedges to serve
- 60g cooked king prawns
- 1 Little Gem lettuce , leaves separated
- ¼ small cucumber , peeled into ribbons
- 4 cherry tomatoes , halved

Method

STEP 1

Heat the oven to 200C/180C fan/gas 6. Slice the pitta into triangles, put on a baking sheet and drizzle over the oil. Bake for 10-15 mins until golden and crisp.

STEP 2

Mix together the Tabasco, ketchup, mayo, yogurt and lime zest and juice. Toss the prawns in the dressing.

STEP 3

Layer the lettuce, cucumber, tomatoes and dressed prawns in a lunchbox or jar. Season, top with the pitta chips and serve with lime wedges.

Ham, mushroom & spinach frittata

Prep:4 mins **Cook:**9 mins

Serves 2

Ingredients

- 1 tsp oil
- 80g chestnut mushrooms , sliced
- 50g ham , diced
- 80g bag spinach
- 4 medium eggs , beaten
- 1 tbsp grated cheddar

Method

STEP 1

Heat the grill to its highest setting. Heat the oil in an ovenproof frying pan over a medium-high heat. Tip in the mushrooms and fry for 2 mins until mostly softened. Stir in the ham and spinach, and cook for 1 min more until the spinach has wilted. Season well with black pepper and a pinch of salt.

STEP 2

Reduce the heat and pour over the eggs. Cook undisturbed for 3 mins until the eggs are mostly set. Sprinkle over the cheese and put under the grill for 2 mins. Serve hot or cold.

Basic lentils

Prep:10 mins **Cook:**45 mins

Makes 6 portions

Ingredients

- 2 tbsp coconut oil
- 2 onions , chopped
- 4 garlic cloves , chopped
- large piece of ginger , chopped
- 300g red split lentils
- 1 tsp turmeric
- 2 tomatoes , roughly chopped
- 1 tsp coriander seeds
- 1 tsp cumin seeds
- 1 tsp black mustard seeds
- 1 lemon , juiced

Method

STEP 1

Melt 1 tbsp coconut oil in a large saucepan. Add the onion and a pinch of salt, and cook for 8 mins. Stir in the garlic and ginger and cook for a few mins more. Add the lentils, turmeric and tomatoes, stir to combine, then pour in 1 litre of water. Bring to the boil, then turn down and simmer for 25-30 mins, stirring occasionally, until the lentils are tender.

STEP 2

Heat the rest of the oil in a frying pan. When it's very hot, add the spices and fry for a min or so until fragrant, then stir them through. Add the lemon juice and season to taste. Will keep for four days in the fridge, or freeze it in batches and use to make our lentil kedgeree, lentil fritters, or spinach dhal with harissa yogurt.

Basic lentils

Prep:10 mins **Cook:**45 mins

Makes 6 portions

Ingredients

- 2 tbsp coconut oil
- 2 onions , chopped
- 4 garlic cloves , chopped
- large piece of ginger , chopped

- 300g red split lentils
- 1 tsp turmeric
- 2 tomatoes , roughly chopped
- 1 tsp coriander seeds
- 1 tsp cumin seeds
- 1 tsp black mustard seeds
- 1 lemon , juiced

Method

STEP 1

Melt 1 tbsp coconut oil in a large saucepan. Add the onion and a pinch of salt, and cook for 8 mins. Stir in the garlic and ginger and cook for a few mins more. Add the lentils, turmeric and tomatoes, stir to combine, then pour in 1 litre of water. Bring to the boil, then turn down and simmer for 25-30 mins, stirring occasionally, until the lentils are tender.

STEP 2

Heat the rest of the oil in a frying pan. When it's very hot, add the spices and fry for a min or so until fragrant, then stir them through. Add the lemon juice and season to taste. Will keep for four days in the fridge, or freeze it in batches and use to make our lentil kedgeree, lentil fritters, or spinach dhal with harissa yogurt.

Chicken & mushroom pancake topping

Prep:5 mins **Cook:**15 mins

Serves 4

Ingredients

- a large knob of butter
- 250g chopped chestnut mushrooms
- 1 crushed garlic clove
- 2 tbsp flour
- 250ml milk
- 2 tsp Dijon mustard
- 2 tbsp mushroom ketchup
- 2 cooked chicken breasts

- a handful chopped parsley

Method

STEP 1

Melt the butter in a pan, add the mushrooms and cook until softened, about 8 mins. Add the garlic and cook for 1 min more, then stir in the flour, milk, mustard and ketchup. Stir for a few mins until you have a thick sauce, then season well.

STEP 2

Shred the chicken and add to the sauce along with the parsley. Top four warm pancakes (see our easy pancakes recipe) with the chicken & mushroom mix and serve.

Raspberry tea ice lollies

Prep: 10 mins plus 4 hrs freezing

Serves 6

Ingredients

- 100g raspberries
- 3 raspberry teabag
- 1 tbsp maple syrup
- juice of 1 lime

Method

STEP 1

Put the raspberries, raspberry tea bags and maple syrup in a bowl, then pour over 350ml boiling water. Leave to infuse for 10 mins, then remove the tea bags, stir in the lime juice and leave to cool. Pour into six ice lolly moulds and freeze for at least 4 hrs, or overnight.

Pea & feta pearl barley stew

Prep: 10 mins **Cook:** 45 mins

Serves 4

Ingredients

- 2 tbsp olive oil
- 2 medium onions , chopped
- 2 garlic cloves , chopped
- zest and juice 2 lemons
- 200g pearl barley , rinsed under cold water
- 700ml vegetable stock
- 200g feta , cut into cubes
- ½ small pack mint , leaves shredded, plus a few whole leaves to serve
- 400g frozen peas , defrosted at room temperature

Method

STEP 1

Heat 1 tbsp oil in a pan or flameproof casserole dish over a medium heat. Add the onion and cook for 3 mins, then add the garlic and lemon zest and fry for another 1 min. Add the pearl barley and the stock. Season, bring to the boil, then simmer for 30 mins, stirring occasionally.

STEP 2

Meanwhile, put the feta in a bowl with the remaining olive oil, half the lemon juice, most of the mint and a good grinding of black pepper. Leave to marinate while the barley cooks.

STEP 3

Remove the lid from the barley and cook for 5 mins more. Increase the heat then add the peas, half the feta and all the feta juices. Cook for 3 mins, then check the seasoning. Divide between four bowls and top with the remaining feta and mint.

Marinated lamb steaks with barley salad

Prep:15 mins **Cook:**30 mins Plus marinating

Serves 2

Ingredients

- 2 tbsp olive oil
- 2 garlic cloves , finely chopped

- pinch dried chilli flakes
- small bunch mint , chopped
- 2 lean lamb leg steaks, about 100g/4oz each, trimmed of any fat
- 100g pearl barley
- 200g broad beans , fresh or frozen, podded and skins removed, if you like
- 100g frozen petits pois
- 1 small red onion , finely chopped
- zest and juice 1 lemon

Method

STEP 1

Mix together 1 tbsp oil, the garlic, chilli, half the mint and some salt and pepper. Rub all over the steaks, then if you have time, leave to marinate for up to 2 hrs.

STEP 2

Cook the pearl barley in boiling, salted water until tender, but not too soft, about 20 mins. Cook the beans and peas in the same pan for the last 2 mins. Drain really well, then tip into a large bowl. Add the red onion, remaining mint, lemon zest and juice, remaining oil, salt and pepper. Toss everything together.

STEP 3

Heat a griddle or frying pan until almost smoking and cook the lamb for 4 mins on each side for pink, or longer if you prefer your meat well done. Divide the barley salad between 2 plates and serve with the grilled lamb, drizzled with any pan juices.

Courgette lasagne

Prep:20 mins **Cook:**1 hr and 25 mins

Serves 6

Ingredients

- 8 plum tomatoes , halved
- 2 garlic cloves , lightly bashed
- 1 tbsp olive oil
- 1 rosemary sprig

- ½ tbsp golden caster sugar
- 2 leeks , sliced into rings
- 20g unsalted butter
- 100g baby spinach
- 500g courgettes , grated
- 10 lasagne sheets
- 250g tub of ricotta
- 125g mozzarella , torn
- 50g parmesan (or vegetarian alternative), grated

Method

STEP 1

Heat oven to 200C/180C fan/gas 6. Put the tomatoes on a baking tray with the garlic, oil, rosemary and a good pinch of seasoning. Bake for 25-30 mins until soft, then discard the rosemary and peel off the garlic skin. Put the tomatoes, garlic and sugar in a blender and blitz a few times until you have a chunky sauce.

STEP 2

Meanwhile, put the leeks in a pan over a low heat, add the butter, season and cook for 7-10 mins or until soft. Add the spinach and courgettes, and cook, covered, for 2 mins until wilted and soft. Set aside.

STEP 3

In a lasagne dish, layer up the ingredients using the tomato sauce first, then some pasta, followed by the ricotta and vegetables. Keep layering until you've used up everything. Finish with a final layer of the vegetables, the mozzarella and the Parmesan. Bake in the oven for 40-45 mins until the sauce has reduced and the top is golden brown.

Veggie olive wraps with mustard vinaigrette

Prep: 10 mins no cook

Serves 1

Ingredients

- 1 carrot , shredded or coarsely grated

- 80g wedge red cabbage , finely shredded
- 2 spring onions , thinly sliced
- 1 courgette , shredded or coarsely grated
- handful basil leaves
- 5 green olives , pitted and halved
- ½ tsp English mustard powder
- 2 tsp extra virgin rapeseed oil
- 1 tbsp cider vinegar
- 1 large seeded tortilla

Method

STEP 1

Mix all the ingredients except for the tortilla and toss well.

STEP 2

Put the tortilla on a sheet of foil and pile the filling along one side of the wrap – it will almost look like too much mixture, but once you start to roll it firmly it will compact. Roll the tortilla from the filling side, folding in the sides as you go. Fold the foil in at the ends to keep stuff inside the wrap. Cut in half and eat straight away. If taking to work, leave whole and wrap up like a cracker in baking parchment.

Rustic vegetable soup

Prep:15 mins **Cook:**30 mins

Serves 4

Ingredients

- 1 tbsp rapeseed oil
- 1 large onion, chopped
- 2 carrots, chopped
- 2 celery sticks, chopped
- 50g dried red lentils
- 1½ l boiling vegetable bouillon (we used Marigold)

- 2 tbsp tomato purée
- 1 tbsp chopped fresh thyme
- 1 leek, finely sliced
- 175g bite-sized cauliflower florets
- 1 courgette, chopped
- 3 garlic cloves, finely chopped
- ½ large Savoy cabbage, stalks removed and leaves chopped
- 1 tbsp basil, chopped

Method

STEP 1

Heat the oil in a large pan with a lid. Add the onion, carrots and celery and fry for 10 mins, stirring from time to time until they are starting to colour a little around the edges. Stir in the lentils and cook for 1 min more.

STEP 2

Pour in the hot bouillon, add the tomato purée and thyme and stir well. Add the leek, cauliflower, courgette, and garlic, bring to the boil, then cover and leave to simmer for 15 mins.

STEP 3

Add the cabbage and basil and cook for 5 mins more until the veg is just tender. Season with pepper, ladle into bowls and serve. Will keep in the fridge for a couple of days. Freezes well. Thaw, then reheat in a pan until piping hot.

Cucumber, pea & lettuce soup

Prep: 5 mins **Cook:** 15 mins

Serves 4

Ingredients

- 1 tsp rapeseed oil
- small bunch spring onions , roughly chopped
- 1 cucumber , roughly chopped
- 1 large round lettuce , roughly chopped
- 225g frozen peas

- 4 tsp vegetable bouillon
- 4 tbsp bio yogurt (optional)
- 4 slices rye bread

Method

STEP 1

Boil 1.4 litres water in a kettle. Heat the oil in a large non-stick frying pan and cook the spring onions for 5 mins, stirring frequently, or until softened. Add the cucumber, lettuce and peas, then pour in the boiled water. Stir in the bouillon, cover and simmer for 10 mins or until the vegetables are soft but still bright green.

STEP 2

Blitz the mixture with a hand blender until smooth. Serve hot or cold, topped with yogurt (if you like), with rye bread alongside.

Penne with broccoli, lemon & anchovies

Prep:10 mins **Cook:**17 mins

Serves 2

Ingredients

- 170g wholemeal penne
- 1 leek , washed and sliced
- 180g broccoli , cut into small florets
- 2 tsp oil from the anchovy can, plus 15g anchovies, chopped
- 1 red pepper , seeded, quartered and sliced
- ½ tsp finely chopped rosemary
- 1 red chilli , seeded and sliced
- 3 garlic cloves , sliced
- ½ lemon , zested and juiced
- 4 tbsp ricotta
- 2 tbsp sunflower seeds

Method

STEP 1

Boil the pasta with the sliced leek for 7 mins, then add the broccoli and boil for 5 mins until everything is just tender.

STEP 2

Meanwhile, heat the oil from the anchovies and fry the red pepper with the rosemary, chilli and garlic in a large non-stick pan for 5 mins until softened.

STEP 3

Drain the pasta, reserving a little water, then tip the pasta and veg into the pan and add the lemon juice and zest, anchovies and ricotta. Toss well over the heat, using the pasta water to moisten. Toss through the sunflower seeds and serve.

Red lentil, chickpea & chilli soup

Prep:10 mins **Cook:**25 mins

Serves 4

Ingredients

- 2 tsp cumin seeds
- large pinch chilli flakes
- 1 tbsp olive oil
- 1 red onion, chopped
- 140g red split lentils
- 850ml vegetable stock or water
- 400g can tomatoes, whole or chopped
- 200g can chickpeas or ½ a can, drained and rinsed (freeze leftovers)
- small bunch coriander, roughly chopped (save a few leaves, to serve)
- 4 tbsp 0% Greek yogurt, to serve

Method

STEP 1

Heat a large saucepan and dry-fry 2 tsp cumin seeds and a large pinch of chilli flakes for 1 min, or until they start to jump around the pan and release their aromas.

STEP 2

Add 1 tbsp olive oil and 1 chopped red onion, and cook for 5 mins.

STEP 3

Stir in 140g red split lentils, 850ml vegetable stock or water and a 400g can tomatoes, then bring to the boil. Simmer for 15 mins until the lentils have softened.

STEP 4

Whizz the soup with a stick blender or in a food processor until it is a rough purée, pour back into the pan and add a 200g can drained and rinsed chickpeas.

STEP 5

Heat gently, season well and stir in a small bunch of chopped coriander, reserving a few leaves to serve. Finish with 4 tbsp 0% Greek yogurt and extra coriander leaves.

Chinese chicken noodle soup with peanut sauce

Prep: 15 mins **Cook:** 30 mins

Serves 2

Ingredients

- 1 tbsp sunflower oil
- 4 skinless boneless chicken thighs
- 1 garlic clove , crushed
- 1 thumb-sized piece ginger , grated
- 500ml chicken stock
- 1 tsp soy sauce
- ½ hispi cabbage , finely sliced
- 150g mushrooms
- 150g straight to wok noodles (we used udon)

For the peanut sauce

- 1 tbsp peanut butter
- 1 tsp soy sauce
- 1 tsp honey
- sriracha or other chilli sauce (optional), to serve

Method

STEP 1

Heat the oil in a saucepan over a medium heat, add the chicken and brown a little, so around 2-3 mins, then add the garlic and ginger and stir to coat the chicken. Fry for a further minute, then pour in the chicken stock and soy, bring to the boil, then reduce to a simmer. Cover with a lid and leave to gently bubble for 25-30 mins until the chicken is tender and pulls apart.

STEP 2

Meanwhile, mix the sauce ingredients with a splash of water. When the chicken is ready, lift it out with a slotted spoon and use two forks to shred it on a plate. Add the cabbage, mushrooms and noodles to the pan, turn up the heat, then stir in the chicken, add a dash of sriracha, if using, and ladle into bowls. Top with a drizzle of the peanut sauce and serve.

Chicken & broccoli potato-topped pie

Prep:35 mins **Cook:**1 hr and 25 mins

Serves 4

Ingredients

- 750g potatoes, peeled and halved
- 250g broccoli, cut into small florets
- 100ml strong chicken stock
- small bunch tarragon, finely chopped (optional)
- 1-2 tsp Dijon mustard
- 100g frozen peas
- 1 tbsp butter

For the chicken base

- 25g butter
- 25g plain flour
- 250ml milk
- 1 tsp olive oil
- 2-3 (depending on size) skinless chicken thigh fillets, cut into cubes
- 1 skinless chicken breast, cut into cubes

- ⅓ onion, very finely chopped (optional)

Method

STEP 1

For the base, melt the butter in a saucepan, stir in the flour and cook for a few mins, stirring all the time. Now, using a whisk or spatula, carefully stir in the milk, a little at a time, making sure the sauce stays smooth. Bring the mixture to a simmer and cook for a couple of mins until it thickens – it will be very thick. Turn the heat right down and keep cooking for 5 mins, stirring often.

STEP 2

Meanwhile, heat the oil in a non-stick frying pan and fry all of the chicken in batches until it starts to colour lightly at the edges. Scoop out each batch of chicken and put it on a plate. Add the onion to the pan if you are using it, and cook over a low heat until soft. Add the chicken and any juices and the onion to the white sauce, fold it in and cook the mixture for a further 15 mins or until the chicken is cooked through. If you're making the base ahead of time, you can leave it to cool at this stage then freeze in an airtight container for up to a month. (Defrost fully before using in the next step.)

STEP 3

Heat oven to 180C/160C fan/gas 4. Cook the potatoes in boiling water for 10 mins, then drain and cool a little before slicing thickly.

STEP 4

Meanwhile, cook the broccoli until tender, then drain. Heat the chicken base with the stock in a pan until it is just beginning to bubble, then stir in the tarragon (if using) and the mustard. Fold in the broccoli and peas. Tip the chicken mixture into a dish and arrange the potato slices on top, then dot the butter over. Bake for 30-35 mins or until golden.

Crab & lemon spaghetti with peas

Prep: 7 mins **Cook:** 12 mins

Serves 2

Ingredients

- 150g wholemeal spaghetti
- 1 tbsp rapeseed oil
- 2 leeks (220g), cut into lengths then long thin strips
- 1 red chilli , deseeded and finely chopped
- 1 garlic clove , finely grated
- 160g frozen peas
- 1 lemon , zested and 1/2 juiced
- 100g fresh white and brown crabmeat (not dressed)

Method

STEP 1

Cook the spaghetti for 12 mins, or following pack instructions, until al dente. Meanwhile, heat the oil in a large frying pan, add the leeks and chilli and cook for 5 mins. Stir in the garlic, peas, lemon zest and juice, then cook for a few mins.

STEP 2

Drain the pasta, then add to the pan with ¼ mug of pasta water and the crab, then toss everything together until well coated. Spoon into shallow bowls and serve.

Garlicky mushroom penne

Prep:20 mins **Cook:**15 mins

Serves 2

Ingredients

- 210g can chickpeas , no need to drain
- 1 tbsp lemon juice
- 1 large garlic clove
- 1 tsp vegetable bouillon
- 2 tsp tahini
- ¼ tsp ground coriander
- 115g wholemeal penne
- 2 tsp rapeseed oil
- 2 red onions , halved and sliced

- 200g closed cup mushrooms , roughly chopped
- ½ lemon , juiced
- generous handful chopped parsley

Method

STEP 1

To make the hummus, tip a 210g can chickpeas with the liquid into a bowl and add 1 tbsp lemon juice, 1 large garlic clove, 1 tsp vegetable bouillon, 2 tsp tahini and ¼ tsp ground coriander.

STEP 2

Blitz to a wet paste with a hand blender, still retaining some texture from the chickpeas.

STEP 3

Cook 115g wholemeal penne pasta according to the pack instructions.

STEP 4

Meanwhile, heat 2 tsp rapeseed oil in a non-stick wok or large frying pan and add 2 halved and sliced red onions and 200g roughly chopped closed cup mushrooms, stirring frequently until softened and starting to caramelise.

STEP 5

Toss together lightly, squeeze over the juice of ½ a lemon and serve, adding a dash of water to loosen the mixture a little if needed. Scatter with a generous handful of chopped parsley.

Banana pancakes

Prep:5 mins **Cook:**5 mins

Serves 2 (makes 4)

Ingredients

- 1 large banana
- 2 medium eggs, beaten
- pinch of baking powder (gluten-free if coeliac)

- splash of vanilla extract
- 1 tsp oil
- 25g pecans, roughly chopped
- 125g raspberries

Method

STEP 1

In a bowl, mash 1 large banana with a fork until it resembles a thick purée.

STEP 2

Stir in 2 beaten eggs, a pinch of baking powder (gluten-free if coeliac) and a splash of vanilla extract.

STEP 3

Heat a large non-stick frying pan or pancake pan over a medium heat and brush with ½ tsp oil.

STEP 4

Using half the batter, spoon two pancakes into the pan, cook for 1-2 mins each side, then tip onto a plate. Repeat the process with another ½ tsp oil and the remaining batter.

STEP 5

Top the pancakes with 25g roughly chopped pecans and 125g raspberries.

Lamb & squash biryani with cucumber raita

Prep:10 mins **Cook:**25 mins

Serves 4

Ingredients

- 4 lean lamb steaks (about 400g), trimmed of all fat, cut into chunks
- 2 garlic cloves , finely grated
- 8 tsp chopped fresh ginger
- 3 tsp ground coriander
- 4 tsp rapeseed oil
- 4 onions , sliced

- 2 red chillies , deseeded and chopped
- 170g brown basmati rice
- 320g diced butternut squash
- 2 tsp cumin seeds
- 2 tsp vegetable bouillon powder
- 20cm length cucumber , grated
- 100ml bio yogurt
- 4 tbsp chopped mint , plus a few extra leaves
- handful coriander , chopped

Method

STEP 1

Mix the lamb with the garlic, 2 tsp chopped ginger and 1 tsp ground coriander and set aside.

STEP 2

Heat 2 tsp oil in a non-stick pan. Add the onions, the remaining ginger and chilli and stir-fry briefly over a high heat so they start to soften. Add the rice and squash and stir over the heat for a few mins. Tip in all the remaining spices, then stir in 500ml boiling water and the bouillon. Cover the pan and simmer for 20 mins.

STEP 3

Meanwhile, mix the cucumber, yogurt and mint together in a bowl to make a raita. Chill half for later.

STEP 4

About 5 mins before the rice is ready, heat the remaining oil in a non-stick frying pan, add the lamb and stir for a few mins until browned but still nice tender. Toss into the spiced rice with the coriander and serve with the raita and a few mint or coriander leaves on top.

Roasted red pepper & tomato soup with ricotta

Prep:10 mins **Cook:**30 mins

Serves 2

Ingredients

- 400g tomatoes , halved
- 1 red onion , quartered
- 2 Romano peppers , roughly chopped
- 2 tbsp good quality olive oil
- 2 garlic cloves , bashed in their skins
- few thyme sprigs
- 1 tbsp red wine vinegar
- 2 tbsp ricotta
- few basil leaves
- 1 tbsp mixed seeds , toasted
- bread , to serve

Method

STEP 1

Heat oven to 200C/180C fan/gas 6. Put the tomatoes, onion and peppers in a roasting tin, toss with the oil and season. Nestle in the garlic and thyme sprigs, then roast for 25-30 mins until all the veg has softened and slightly caramelised. Squeeze the garlic cloves out of their skins into the tin, strip the leaves off the thyme and discard the stalks and garlic skins. Mix the vinegar into the tin then blend everything in a bullet blender or using a stick blender, adding enough water to loosen to your preferred consistency (we used around 150ml).

STEP 2

Reheat the soup if necessary, taste for seasoning, then spoon into two bowls and top each with a spoonful of ricotta, a few basil leaves, the seeds and a drizzle of oil. Serve with bread for dunking.

Ginger & soy sea bass parcels

Prep:30 mins **Cook:**15 mins

Serves 4

Ingredients

- 100ml shaohsing rice wine or dry sherry
- 100ml light soy sauce
- 1 small bunch of spring onions , finely sliced

- 2 garlic cloves , finely chopped
- thumb-sized piece fresh ginger , finely chopped
- 4 sea bass fillets, scaled (about 100g each)
- 3 pak choi , each quartered
- 1 large carrot , shredded into fine strips
- 2 red chillies , 4 spring onions, and thumb-sized piece ginger, cut into fine strips, to serve

Method

STEP 1

In a jug, mix together the wine or sherry with the soy, spring onions, garlic and ginger, then set aside. Lightly score the skin of each sea bass fillet a couple of times.

STEP 2

Lay a square of foil on your work surface with a square of baking parchment the same size on top. Put 3 pak choi quarters just off centre of the paper and top with a quarter of the shredded carrot followed by a sea bass fillet, skin-side up. Spoon over a quarter of the ginger, onion and garlic mixture (don't add the rice wine and soy mixture yet). Fold over the parcel so it becomes a triangle, then, from left to right, begin to seal it by scrunching the edges together. Continue all the way around until there is just a little hole at the end. Pour a quarter of the soy mix through the hole. Scrunch the remaining bit to seal and place on a baking tray. Repeat until all the fish are wrapped, sauced and sealed. Can be prepared a day ahead and chilled.

STEP 3

Heat oven to 200C/180C fan/gas 6 and cook the fish on the tray for 15 mins. Remove from the oven and divide the parcels between four warmed plates. Let your guests open them up themselves so they get a hit of aromatic steam before they tuck in. Pass around some chilli, spring onion and ginger strips to sprinkle over.

Vegetarian bean pot with herby breadcrumbs

Prep: 10 mins **Cook:** 35 mins

Serves 2

Ingredients

- 1 slice crusty bread

- ½ small pack parsley leaves
- ½ lemon , zested
- 2 tbsp olive oil
- pinch chilli flakes (optional)
- 2 leeks , rinsed and chopped into half-moons
- 2 carrots , thinly sliced
- 2 celery sticks , thinly sliced
- 1 fennel bulb , thinly sliced
- 2 large garlic cloves , chopped
- 1 tbsp tomato purée
- few thyme sprigs
- 150ml white wine
- 400g can cannellini beans , drained

Method

STEP 1

Toast the bread, then tear into pieces and put in a food processor with the parsley, lemon zest, ½ tbsp olive oil, a good pinch of salt and pepper and the chilli flakes, if using. Blitz to breadcrumbs. Set aside.

STEP 2

Heat the remaining oil in a pan and add the leeks, carrots, celery and fennel along with a splash of water and a pinch of salt. Cook over a medium heat for 10 mins until soft, then add the garlic and tomato purée. Cook for 1 min more, then add the thyme and white wine. Leave to bubble for a minute, then add the beans. Fill the can halfway with water and pour into the pot.

STEP 3

Bring the cassoulet to the boil, then turn down the heat and leave to simmer for 15 mins before removing the thyme sprigs. Mash half the beans to thicken the stew. Season to taste, then divide between bowls and top with the herby breadcrumbs to serve.

Banana & cinnamon pancakes with blueberry compote

Prep: 10 mins **Cook:** 15 mins

Serves 4

Ingredients

- 65g wholemeal flour
- 1 tsp ground cinnamon , plus extra for sprinkling
- 2 egg , plus 2 egg whites
- 100ml whole milk
- 1 small banana , mashed
- ½ tbsp rapeseed oil
- 320g blueberries
- few mint leaves , to serve

Method

STEP 1

Tip the flour and cinnamon into a bowl, then break in the whole eggs, pour in the milk and whisk together until smooth. Stir in the banana. In a separate bowl, whisk the egg whites until light and fluffy, but not completely stiff, then fold into the pancake mix until evenly incorporated.

STEP 2

Heat a small amount of oil in a large non-stick frying pan, then add a quarter of the pancake mix, swirl to cover the base of the pan and cook until set and golden. Carefully turn the pancake over with a palette knife and cook the other side. Transfer to a plate, then carry on with the rest of the batter until you have four.

STEP 3

To make the compote, tip the berries in a non-stick pan and heat gently until the berries just burst but hold their shape. Serve two warm pancakes with half the berries, then scatter with the mint leaves and sprinkle with a little cinnamon. Chill the remaining pancakes and compote and serve the next day. You can reheat them in the microwave or in a pan.

Black-eyed bean mole with salsa

Prep:15 mins **Cook:**5 mins - 8 mins

Serves 2

Ingredients

For the salsa

- 1 red onion , finely chopped
- 2 large tomatoes , chopped
- 2 tbsp fresh coriander
- ½ lime , zest and juice

For the mole

- 2 tsp rapeseed oil
- 1 red onion , halved and sliced
- 1 garlic clove , finely grated
- 1 tsp ground coriander
- 1 tsp mild chilli powder
- ½ tsp ground cinnamon
- 400g can black-eyed beans in water
- 2 tsp cocoa
- 1 tsp vegetable bouillon
- 1 tbsp tomato purée

Method

STEP 1

Tip all the salsa ingredients into a bowl and stir together.

STEP 2

For the mole, heat the oil in a non-stick pan, add the onion and garlic and fry stirring frequently until softened. Tip in the spices, stir then add the contents of the can of beans with the cocoa, bouillon and tomato purée. Cook, stirring frequently to make quite a thick sauce.

STEP 3

Spoon into shallow bowls, top with the salsa and serve.

Salmon pasta salad with lemon & capers

Prep:10 mins **Cook:**20 mins

Serves 2

Ingredients

- 85g wholewheat penne
- 1 tbsp rapeseed oil
- 1 large red pepper , roughly chopped
- 2 frozen, skinless wild salmon fillets (about 120g each)
- 1 lemon , zested and juiced
- 2 garlic cloves , finely grated
- 1 shallot , very finely chopped
- 2 tbsp capers
- 6 pitted Kalamata olives , sliced
- 1 tsp extra virgin olive oil
- 2 handfuls rocket

Method

STEP 1

Cook the pasta following pack instructions. Meanwhile, heat the rapeseed oil in a frying pan, add the pepper, cover and leave for about 5 mins until it softens and starts to char a little. Stir, then push the pepper to one side and add the salmon. Cover and fry for 8-10 mins until just cooked.

STEP 2

Meanwhile, mix the lemon zest and juice in a large bowl with the garlic, shallot, capers and olives.

STEP 3

Add the cooked pepper and salmon to the bowl. Drain the pasta and add it too, with black pepper and the olive oil. Toss everything together, flaking the salmon as you do so. If eating now, toss through the rocket; if packing a lunch, leave to cool, then put in a container with the rocket on top and mix through just before eating.

Avocado hummus & crudités

Prep:10 mins No cook

Serves 2

Ingredients

- 1 avocado , peeled and stoned
- 210g chickpeas , drained
- 1 garlic clove , crushed
- pinch chilli flakes , plus extra to serve
- 1 lime , juiced
- handful coriander leaves
- 2 carrots , cut into strips
- 2 mixed peppers , cut into strips
- 160g sugar snap peas

Method

STEP 1

Blitz together the avocado, chickpeas, garlic, chilli flakes and lime juice, and season to taste. Top the hummus with the coriander leaves and a few more chilli flakes, and serve with the carrot, pepper and sugar snap crudités. Make the night before for a great take-to-work lunch.

Avocado hummus & crudités

Prep: 10 mins No cook

Serves 2

Ingredients

- 1 avocado , peeled and stoned
- 210g chickpeas , drained
- 1 garlic clove , crushed
- pinch chilli flakes , plus extra to serve
- 1 lime , juiced
- handful coriander leaves
- 2 carrots , cut into strips
- 2 mixed peppers , cut into strips
- 160g sugar snap peas

Method

STEP 1

Blitz together the avocado, chickpeas, garlic, chilli flakes and lime juice, and season to taste. Top the hummus with the coriander leaves and a few more chilli flakes, and serve with the carrot, pepper and sugar snap crudités. Make the night before for a great take-to-work lunch.

Creamy tomato courgetti

Prep:1 min **Cook:**3 mins

Serves 2

Ingredients

- 4 slices of Parma ham
- ½ small pack basil
- 350g tomato and mascarpone sauce
- 250g pack courgetti

Method

STEP 1

Roughly tear the ham and basil. Heat a frying pan over a medium heat and dry-fry the ham until crisp. Transfer to a plate with a slotted spoon. Add the sauce to the pan and cook for 1-2 mins, then toss in the courgetti. Cook for 1 min more until warmed through. Divide between bowls, then top with the ham and basil.

Beef bulgogi stir-fry

Prep:10 mins **Cook:**10 mins

Serves 4

Ingredients

- 4cm/1 ½in piece of ginger
- 4 tbsp soy sauce
- 4 tbsp mirin

- 3 garlic cloves
- 2 tbsp chopped pineapple
- 2 tsp red chilli flakes or Korean chilli powder
- 3 tbsp golden caster sugar
- 3 tsp sesame oil
- 500g sirloin or rump steak , trimmed of fat and sliced
- 1 large onion , cut into half moons
- 1 tbsp toasted sesame seeds
- 200g cooked basmati rice
- chopped spring onions , to serve

Method

STEP 1

Put the ginger, soy, mirin, garlic, pineapple, chilli flakes, sugar and 1 tsp of the sesame oil in a food processor and blend until fine. Pour the marinade into a bowl, add the meat, mix well and leave to sit while you prepare the onion.

STEP 2

Heat the remaining sesame oil in a large wok or frying pan until very hot. Add the onion and stir-fry for a few mins. Add the beef and the marinade, stirring constantly until it's cooked through, about 5 mins. Sprinkle with the sesame seeds and serve with rice and chopped spring onions.

BBQ salad pizza

Prep:25 mins **Cook:**20 mins Plus rising time

Serves 2-3

Ingredients

For the pizza dough

- strong white bread flour , plus extra for dusting
- ½ tsp easy or fast-action dried yeast

For the topping

- 3 Little Gem lettuces , cut in half
- 6 spring onions
- 200g Tenderstem broccoli
- oil , for brushing
- 30g walnuts , toasted and roughly chopped

For the dressing

- 75ml buttermilk (if you can't find any, squeeze a little lemon juice into milk and leave for 5 mins to sour)
- 2 tbsp thick Greek yogurt
- 1 tsp Dijon mustard
- ½ garlic clove , crushed
- 1 lemon , zested and juiced

Method

STEP 1

To make the pizza dough, combine the flour, yeast and a big pinch of salt in a large bowl. Pour in 120ml warm water and knead together with well-floured hands to form a smooth dough. Put the dough back in its bowl, cover with a tea towel and leave somewhere warm to double in size. Can be made the night before and kept chilled overnight.

STEP 2

For the buttermilk dressing, whisk together all the ingredients, adding lemon juice and some seasoning to taste. The dressing can be made the day before.

STEP 3

Get your barbecue searingly hot. Brush the broccoli, spring onions and the cut side of the lettuce with a little oil, then put all the vegetables on the barbecue and cook until charred – broccoli will take the longest, between 8-10 mins. Have a plate ready so you can remove them when they're cooked.

STEP 4

On a lightly floured surface, roll the pizza dough into a circle, about 30cm in diameter. Flour a large piece of foil, put the dough on top and carefully place on the barbecue. Put the lid on the barbecue and cook the dough, with the lid on throughout, for 6-8 mins, flipping halfway, or until cooked through – it may take slightly longer if your barbecue has lost some heat. Pile the charred veg on top of the dough, drizzle over some of the dressing (leaving some to dip the crusts), then scatter over the toasted walnuts and lemon zest to serve.

Courgetti bolognese

Prep: 15 mins **Cook:** 1 hr

Serves 4

Ingredients

- 2 tbsp olive oil
- 500g turkey mince (thigh or breast)
- 1 large onion , finely chopped
- 1 garlic clove , crushed
- 2 large carrots , peeled and diced
- 150g pack button mushrooms , roughly chopped
- 1 tbsp tomato purée
- 2 x 400g cans chopped tomatoes
- 2 chicken stock cubes
- 1 tbsp soy sauce
- 4 large courgettes
- grated pecorino or parmesan , to serve
- handful basil leaves

Method

STEP 1

Heat 1 tbsp of the olive oil in a large saucepan and add the turkey mince. Fry until browned, then scoop into a bowl and set aside.

STEP 2

Add the onion to the pan and cook on a low heat for 8-10 mins until tender. Then add the garlic, stirring for 1 min or so, followed by the carrot and the mushrooms, stirring for about 3 mins, until softened. Tip the turkey mince back into the pan, add the tomato purée, give everything a quick stir and tip in the chopped tomatoes. Fill 1 can with water and pour into the pan. Crumble over the chicken stock cubes and bring to the boil. Once boiling, lower the heat and simmer for about 1 hr, until the sauce has thickened and the veg is tender.

STEP 3

When the bolognese is nearly ready, stir through the soy sauce and some seasoning. Spiralize your courgettes on the large noodle attachment. Heat a large frying pan with the remaining 1 tbsp olive oil and add your courgetti. Cook until slightly softened, for 2-3 mins. Season with salt and serve topped with the turkey bolognese, grated pecorino and basil leaves.

Slow-cooker ham with sticky ginger glaze

Prep: 20 mins **Cook:** 7 hrs and 20 mins

Serves 6 - 8

Ingredients

- 1 onion, thickly sliced
- 10 cloves, plus extra for studding
- 1 medium gammon joint, approx 1.3kg
- 1.5 litre bottle ginger beer
- 1 tbsp English mustard
- 3 tbsp ginger preserve

Method

STEP 1

Put the onion and 10 cloves in the base of the slow cooker then nestle in the gammon joint. Pour over the ginger beer then cover and cook on LOW for 7 hours until the gammon is tender, but still holding its shape. You can cool then chill the gammon at this stage if you prefer.

STEP 2

Heat the oven to 200C/180C fan/ gas 6. Carefully remove the skin from the gammon leaving a layer of fat behind. Score the fat in a diamond pattern with a sharp knife, making sure you don't cut into the meat, then stud the centre of each diamond with cloves.

STEP 3

Mix the mustard and ginger preserve in a bowl, spoon or brush over the gammon then bake for 20 mins until golden and sticky. If roasting from cold you will need to add another 20 mins to the cooking time.

Chunky butternut mulligatawny

Prep:25 mins **Cook:**40 mins

Serves 6

Ingredients

- 2 tbsp olive or rapeseed oil
- 2 onions , finely chopped
- 2 dessert apples , peeled and finely chopped
- 3 celery sticks, finely chopped
- ½ small butternut squash , peeled, seeds removed, chopped into small pieces
- 2-3 heaped tbsp gluten-free curry powder (depending on how spicy you like it)
- 1 tbsp ground cinnamon
- 1 tbsp nigella seeds (also called black onion or kalonji seeds)
- 2 x 400g cans chopped tomatoes
- 1 ½l gluten-free chicken or vegetable stock
- 140g basmati rice
- small pack parsley , chopped
- 3 tbsp mango chutney , plus a little to serve, if you like (optional)
- natural yogurt , to serve

Method

STEP 1

Heat the oil in your largest saucepan. Add the onions, apples and celery with a pinch of salt. Cook for 10 mins, stirring now and then, until softened. Add the butternut squash, curry powder, cinnamon, nigella seeds and a grind of black pepper. Cook for 2 mins more, then stir in the tomatoes and stock. Cover with a lid and simmer for 15 mins.

STEP 2

By now the vegetables should be tender but not mushy. Stir in the rice, pop the lid back on and simmer for another 12 mins until the rice is cooked through. Taste and add more seasoning if needed. Stir through the parsley and mango chutney, then serve in bowls with yogurt and extra mango chutney on top, if you like.

Prawn & pak choi stir-fry

Prep: 5 mins **Cook:** 6 mins

Serves 2

Ingredients

- 2 tbsp sesame oil
- 100g mangetout
- 1 carrot , finely sliced
- 200g pak choi , washed and sliced
- 2 spring onions , sliced on the diagonal
- 300g straight-to-wok egg noodles
- 150g cooked king prawns
- 2 tbsp soy sauce , plus extra to serve, (optional)
- 1 tbsp sesame seeds , toasted
- 1 red chilli , sliced, to serve (optional)

Method

STEP 1

Heat 1 tbsp sesame oil in a large wok or frying pan over a medium-high heat and toss in the mangetout and carrot. Cook for a few mins until starting to soften and brown, then add the pak choi and spring onions. Add the noodles and prawns, use tongs to combine, and warm through.

STEP 2

Pour in the soy sauce and remaining sesame oil, and toss to coat. Just before serving, scatter over the sesame seeds and chilli. Serve with extra soy sauce, if you like.

Asian pulled chicken salad

Prep: 20 mins No cook

Serves 5

Ingredients

- 1 small roasted chicken , about 1kg
- ½ red cabbage , cored and finely sliced
- 3 carrots , coarsley grated or finely shredded
- 5 spring onions , finely sliced on the diagonal
- 2 red chillies , halved and thinly sliced
- small bunch coriander , roughly chopped, including stalks
- 2 heaped tbsp roasted salted peanuts , roughly crushed

For the dressing

- 3 ½ tbsp hoisin sauce
- 1 ½ tbsp toasted sesame oil

Method

STEP 1

Combine the dressing ingredients in a small bowl and set aside.

STEP 2

Remove all the meat from the chicken, shred into large chunks and pop in a large bowl. Add the cabbage, carrots, spring onions, chillies and half the coriander. Toss together with the dressing and pile onto a serving plate, then scatter over the remaining coriander and peanuts.

Baked ginger & spinach sweet potato

Prep:10 mins **Cook:**45 mins

Serves 1

Ingredients

- 1 sweet potato
- 2 tsp oil
- ½ onion , finely chopped
- 1 garlic clove , crushed

- small knob of ginger , grated
- 1-2 tsp curry paste (use what you have or buy a Madras or red curry paste)
- knob of butter
- handful of spinach

Method

STEP 1

Heat oven to 200C/180C fan/gas 6. Prick the potato and bake it for 40-45 mins or until soft when you squeeze the sides.

STEP 2

Meanwhile, heat the oil in a small frying pan and fry the onion until softened, add the garlic and cook for 1 min, then add the ginger and curry paste and cook for another min. Stir in the butter and spinach, and continue stirring until the spinach wilts. Season well.

STEP 3

Cut open the top of the sweet potato, scoop out some of the flesh, add it to the mix in the pan and stir through, then spoon the mixture back into the potato.

Goat's cheese, tomato & olive triangles

Prep:5 mins No cook

Serves 2

Ingredients

- 3 triangular bread thins
- 50g soft goat's cheese
- 2 x 5cm lengths of cucumber , thinly sliced lengthways
- 3 tomatoes , sliced
- 4 Kalamata olives , finely chopped
- 2 small handfuls rocket leaves

Method

STEP 1

Follow our triangular bread-thins recipe to make your own.

STEP 2

Cut the bread thins in half, put cut-side up and spread with the goat's cheese. Top with the cucumber and tomato, then scatter over the olives and top with the rocket. Eat straight away or pack into lunchboxes for later.

Healthy stuffing balls

Prep: 20 mins **Cook:** 45 mins

Serves 8, makes about 12

Ingredients

- 1 tbsp olive oil
- 1 large onion , finely chopped
- 2 sticks celery , stringed and finely chopped
- 2 garlic cloves , finely chopped
- 15g dried apricots , roughly chopped
- 75g peeled chestnuts
- 75g almonds
- 100g wholemeal bread , crusts removed and roughly torn (about 6 slices)
- large bunch parsley , chopped
- large pinch dried sage
- 1 egg

Method

STEP 1

Heat oven to 200C/180C fan/gas 6. Gently heat the oil in a shallow saucepan then add the onion, celery and garlic. Keep everything sizzling on a medium heat for 15 mins until soft. Tip into a food processor with the rest of the ingredients, except the egg, plus a small pinch of salt, if you like. Pulse until everything is chopped, then add the egg and pulse until combined. Use wet hands to roll the mixture into walnut-sized balls, then place on a baking sheet lined with baking parchment.

STEP 2

Bake in the oven for 25-30 mins until golden and hot through. Will freeze for up to three months; defrost fully before reheating.

Scrambled egg & feta hash

Prep: 7 mins **Cook:** 8 mins

Serves 1

Ingredients

- 2 tbsp coconut oil
- 90g cherry tomatoes , halved
- 4 spring onions , chopped
- 60g feta , cut into small cubes
- 3 eggs , beaten
- 1 tsp snipped chives
- 110g spinach

Method

STEP 1

Heat the oil in a non-stick pan on a low-medium heat. Add the tomatoes and spring onions, and cook gently for 3-4 mins until softened.

STEP 2

Add the feta and cook for 1 min to warm through, then pour in the eggs and chives. Season with pepper and keep stirring to scramble the eggs. Put a handful of the spinach on a plate and top with the eggs. Serve the rest of the spinach on the side.

Sweet potato jackets with pomegranate & celeriac slaw

Prep: 5 mins **Cook:** 35 mins - 40 mins

Serves 2

Ingredients

- 2 sweet potatoes (about 195g each)
- 90g pomegranate seeds
- 8 walnut halves , broken
- small handful coriander , chopped
- 120g pot bio yogurt

For the slaw

- 1 small red onion , halved and thinly sliced
- 160g peeled celeriac , thinly sliced into matchsticks
- 2 celery sticks , chopped
- 1 tbsp lemon juice
- 1 tbsp rapeseed oil
- 2 tsp balsamic vinegar
- 0.5 - 1 tsp English mustard powder (optional)
- 2 tbsp chopped parsley

Method

STEP 1

Heat oven to 200C/180C fan/gas 6. Roast the sweet potatoes for 35-40 mins until a knife slides in easily.

STEP 2

Meanwhile, pour boiling water over the onion and leave for 5 mins, then rinse under the cold tap and pat dry with kitchen paper. Tip into a bowl and add the celeriac and celery with all but 4 tbsp yogurt along with the remaining slaw ingredients and toss together.

STEP 3

Cut into the potatoes and gently squeeze to open them. Top with the remaining yogurt, pomegranate and walnuts. Scatter over the coriander. Serve with the slaw.

Creamy leek & bean soup

Prep:10 mins **Cook:**20 mins

Serves 4

Ingredients

- 1 tbsp rapeseed oil
- 600g leeks , well washed and thinly sliced
- 1l hot vegetable bouillon
- 2 x 400g cans cannellini beans , drained
- 2 large garlic cloves , finely grated
- 100g baby spinach
- 150ml full-fat milk

Method

STEP 1

Heat the oil in a large pan, add the leeks and cook on a low-medium heat for 5 mins. Pour in the bouillon, tip in the beans, cover and simmer for 10 mins.

STEP 2

Stir in the garlic and spinach, cover the pan and cook for 5 mins more until the spinach has wilted but still retains its fresh green colour.

STEP 3

Add the milk and plenty of pepper, and blitz with a stick blender until smooth. Ladle into bowls and chill the remainder.

Honey & orange roast sea bass with lentils

Prep: 15 mins **Cook:** 10 mins

Serves 2

Ingredients

- 2 large skin-on sea bass fillets (or other white fish - see tip)
- zest and juice ½ orange
- 2 tsp clear honey
- 2 tsp wholegrain mustard
- 2 tbsp olive oil
- 250g pouch ready-to-eat puy lentils

- 100g watercress
- small bunch parsley, chopped
- small bunch dill, chopped

Method

STEP 1

Heat oven to 200C/180C fan/gas 6. Place each sea bass fillet, skin-side down, on individual squares of foil. Mix together the orange zest, honey, mustard, 1 tbsp olive oil and some seasoning, and drizzle it over the fillets. Pull the sides of the foil up and twist the edges together to make individual parcels. Place the parcels on a baking tray and bake in the oven for 10 mins until the fish is just cooked and flakes easily when pressed with a knife.

STEP 2

Warm the lentils following pack instructions, then mix with the orange juice, remaining oil, the watercress, herbs and seasoning. Divide the lentils between 2 plates and top each with a sea bass fillet. Drizzle over any roasting juices that are caught in the foil and serve immediately.

Chicken and mushrooms

Prep:15 mins **Cook:**25 mins

Serves 4

Ingredients

- 2 tbsp olive oil
- 500g boneless, skinless chicken thigh
- flour, for dusting
- 50g cubetti di pancetta
- 300g small button mushroom
- 2 large shallots, chopped
- 250ml chicken stock
- 1 tbsp white wine vinegar
- 50g frozen pea
- small handful parsley, finely chopped

Method

STEP 1

Heat 1 tbsp oil in a frying pan. Season and dust the chicken with flour, brown on all sides. Remove. Fry the pancetta and mushrooms until softened, then remove.

STEP 2

Add the final tbsp oil and cook shallots for 5 mins. Add the stock and vinegar, bubble for 1-2 mins. Return the chicken, pancetta and mushrooms and cook for 15 mins. Add the peas and parsley and cook for 2 mins more, then serve.

Spicy meatball tagine with bulgur & chickpeas

Prep:10 mins **Cook:**45 mins plus chilling

Serves 4

Ingredients

- 2 onions , 1 quartered, 1 halved and sliced
- 2 tbsp tomato purée
- 2 garlic cloves
- 1 egg
- 1 tbsp chilli powder
- 500g pack extra-lean beef mince
- 2 tsp rapeseed oil
- 4 large carrots , cut into batons
- 1 tsp ground cumin
- 2 tsp ground coriander
- 400g can chopped tomatoes
- 1 lemon , zest removed with a potato peeler, then chopped
- 12 Kalamata olives , chopped
- 1 tbsp vegetable bouillon powder
- ⅓ pack fresh coriander , chopped

For the bulgur

- 200g bulgur wheat
- 400g can chickpeas

168

- 2 tsp vegetable bouillon powder
- 2 tsp ground coriander

Method

STEP 1

Put the quartered onion in the food processor and process to finely chop it. Add the minced beef, 1 tbsp tomato purée, the garlic, egg and chilli powder and blitz to make a smoothish paste. Divide the mixture into 26 even-sized pieces and roll into balls.

STEP 2

Heat the oil in a large frying pan and cook the meatballs for about 5-10 mins to lightly brown them. Tip from the pan onto a plate.

STEP 3

Now add the sliced onion and carrots to the pan and stir fry briefly in the pan juices to soften them a little. Add the spices and pour in the tomatoes with 1 ½ cans of water then stir in the chopped lemon zest, remaining tomato purée, olives and bouillon powder. Return the meatballs to the pan then cover and cook for 15 mins until the carrots are just tender. Stir in the coriander.

STEP 4

While the tagine is cooking, tip the bulgur into a pan with the chickpeas and water from the can. Add 2 cans of water, the bouillon and coriander. Cover and cook for 10 mins until the bulgur is tender and the liquid had been absorbed. If you're doing the Healthy Diet Plan (serving two people), serve half with half of the tagine and chill the remainder for another night if you like.

Moroccan harira

Prep:15 mins **Cook:**40 mins

Serves 4

Ingredients

- 1-2 tbsp rapeseed oil
- 2 large onions , finely chopped
- 4 garlic cloves , chopped
- 2 tsp turmeric

- 2 tsp cumin
- ½ tsp cinnamon
- 2 red chillies , deseeded and sliced
- 500g carton passata
- 1.7l reduced-salt vegetable bouillon
- 175dried green lentils
- 2 carrots , chopped into small pieces
- 1 sweet potato , peeled and diced
- 5 celery sticks , chopped into small pieces
- ⅔ small pack coriander , few sprigs reserved, the rest chopped
- 1 lemon , cut into 4 wedges, to serve

Method

STEP 1

Heat the oil in a large non-stick sauté pan over a medium heat and fry the onions and garlic until starting to soften. Tip in the spices and chilli, stir briefly, then pour in the passata and stock. Add the lentils, carrots, sweet potato and celery, and bring to the boil.

STEP 2

Cover the pan and leave to simmer for 30 mins, then cook uncovered for a further 5-10 mins until the vegetables and lentils are tender. Stir in the chopped coriander and serve in bowls with lemon wedges for squeezing over, and the reserved coriander sprinkled over.

Chicken piccata with garlicky greens & new potatoes

Prep:5 mins **Cook:**15 mins

Serves 2

Ingredients

- 200g new potatoes , halved or quartered
- 300g green beans , trimmed
- 200g spring greens , shredded
- 2 skinless chicken breasts

- 3 tsp olive oil
- 100ml chicken stock or water
- 1 tbsp drained capers
- 1 lemon , zested and juiced
- 2 small garlic cloves , sliced
- 1 tbsp grated parmesan

Method

STEP 1

Cook the new potatoes in a large pan of boiling salted water for 8-10 mins until tender. Add the green beans and spring greens for the last 3 mins. Drain, then separate the greens from the potatoes.

STEP 2

While the potatoes are cooking, cut the chicken breasts through the centre lengthways, leaving one side attached so it opens out like a book. Brush each one with 1 tsp of the olive oil, then season.

STEP 3

Heat a large frying pan over a medium-high heat and cook the chicken for 4 mins on each side until golden. Pour over the stock, capers, lemon juice and zest, then simmer gently for a few minutes to reduce. Add the cooked potatoes and simmer for another minute.

STEP 4

Heat the remaining 1 tsp oil in another frying pan and fry the garlic for 1 min until lightly golden and fragrant. Tip in the drained greens, and toss in the garlicky oil. Season, then scatter over the parmesan and serve with the chicken and potatoes.

Apple & penne slaw with walnuts

Prep: 15 mins **Cook:** 12 mins

Serves 4

Ingredients

- 200g wholemeal penne

- 2 x 150g pots bio yogurt
- 4 tsp sherry vinegar
- 2 tsp English mustard powder
- 4 spring onions , finely chopped
- 6 celery sticks (320g), finely chopped
- 400g and 210g cans chickpeas , drained
- 30g raisins
- 2 apples
- 12 walnut halves (35g), broken up
- 8 crisp lettuce leaves from an iceberg lettuce

Method

STEP 1

Boil the penne for 12 mins until al dente. Meanwhile, make a dressing by mixing the yogurt with the vinegar, mustard and spring onions.

STEP 2

Add the celery, penne, chickpeas and raisins to the dressing and stir until everything is well coated. If you're following our Healthy Diet Plan, chop 1 apple and add to half the salad with half the nuts and serve with half of the crisp lettuce leaves, either as a base or as wraps. Chill the remainder for up to three days, then add the apple, nuts and lettuce on the day you're eating it. If you do it ahead, the nuts will soften and the apples will turn brown.

Sweet potato, coconut & lemongrass soup with coriander sambal

Prep: 15 mins **Cook:** 30 mins

Serves 4

Ingredients

- 2 tbsp groundnut oil
- 4 spring onions , sliced
- 2 large garlic cloves , sliced
- 2 lemongrass stalks , outer leaves removed and stalk finely chopped

- finger-sized piece ginger , sliced
- 900g sweet potatoes , peeled and chopped into small pieces
- 215ml coconut milk
- 285ml vegetable stock (we used Bouillon)
- 1 green chilli , deseeded
- 1 tsp caster sugar
- 2 limes , juiced
- 1 small pack coriander

Method

STEP 1

Heat the oil in a large pan, then add the spring onions, garlic, lemongrass and three-quarters of the ginger and cook for 2 mins until aromatic, then tip in the sweet potato. Give everything a good mix so the sweet potato is well coated, then add the coconut milk, stock and 500ml water. Bring to the boil, then simmer for around 25 mins until the sweet potato is cooked through.

STEP 2

Meanwhile, tip the remaining ginger, the chilli, sugar, three-quarters of the lime juice and most of the coriander (reserving a few leaves for a garnish) into a food processor and blitz until smooth. Transfer the sambal to a small jug and set aside.

STEP 3

Blitz the soup with a hand blender until smooth, then season to taste with the remaining lime juice and some salt and pepper. Divide the soup between bowls and top with the coriander sambal. Garnish with the reserved coriander leaves.

Healthy gravy

Prep:5 mins **Cook:**25 mins

Serves 8

Ingredients

- 1 tsp sunflower oil
- 1 large onion , chopped
- 3 large carrots , chopped

- 1 tbsp ketchup
- handful dried porcini mushrooms
- 3 tbsp balsamic vinegar
- 1l low-salt vegetable stock , or chicken stock if not making it vegetarian
- 1 tbsp cornflour

Method

STEP 1

Heat the oil in a saucepan then add the vegetables and cook them over a medium-high heat for 10-15 mins to brown – if they burn at the edges, then all the better. Stir in the ketchup and dried mushrooms and cook together until everything becomes sticky, then splash in the vinegar. Stir in the stock and season with a pinch of salt, if you like. Bring to the boil, then simmer gently for 20 mins.

STEP 2

Using a hand blender, blitz to create a thin soup-like consistency, then pass through a sieve into another saucepan and bring to the simmer. Slake the cornflour with a splash of water, then pour into the liquid and continue to cook until thickened. Serve straightaway, chill, or freeze for reheating at a later date. Can be frozen for up to three months in an airtight container.

Oregano chicken & squash traybake

Prep:5 mins **Cook:**50 mins

Serves 4

Ingredients

- 180g pack grilled artichokes
- 1½ tbsp olive oil
- 1 tsp dried oregano
- 2 tsp cumin seeds
- 8 chicken drumsticks
- 1 butternut squash, cut into chunks (leave the skin on – it adds flavour)
- 150g mixed olives of your choice, roughly chopped
- large handful rocket

Method

STEP 1

Heat oven to 220C/200C fan/gas 6. Measure out 1½ tbsp of oil from the grilled artichoke pack. Mix this with the olive oil, oregano and cumin. Put the chicken drumsticks and squash in a large roasting tin, toss in the flavoured oil and some seasoning.

STEP 2

Roast in the oven for 45 mins until tender and golden, then tip the artichokes and olives into the pan. Give everything a good mix, then return to the oven for 5 mins to warm through. Stir through the rocket and serve.

Watermelon lollies

Prep:15 mins Plus at least 4 hours freezing

Serves 6 - 8

Ingredients

- 1 small watermelon
- 3 kiwis

Method

STEP 1

Halve 1 small watermelon and scoop the flesh out of one half into a bowl (you need about 375-400g). Pick out any black seeds. Purée the flesh using a hand blender or in a liquidiser. Fill ice lolly moulds three-quarters full with the purée, push the sticks in if you are using them, and freeze for at least 3 hrs, or overnight. Tip any remaining purée into an ice cube tray and freeze it.

STEP 2

Peel 3 kiwis and cut the green flesh away from the white core, discarding the core. Purée the flesh. Add a layer of about 4-5mm to the top of each lolly and refreeze for 1 hr. Add some green food colouring to the rest of the purée to darken it to the same colour as the watermelon rind. Pour a very thin layer onto the top of each lolly and freeze until you want to eat them.

Lamb dopiaza with broccoli rice

Prep:20 mins **Cook:**1 hr and 30 mins

Serves 2

Ingredients

- 225g lamb leg steaks , trimmed of excess fat and cut into 2.5cm/ 1in chunks
- 50g full-fat natural bio yogurt , plus 4 tbsp to serve
- 1 tbsp medium curry powder
- 2 tsp cold-pressed rapeseed oil
- 2 medium onions , 1 thinly sliced, 1 cut into 5 wedges
- 2 garlic cloves , peeled and finely sliced
- 1 tbsp ginger , peeled and finely chopped
- 1 small red chilli , finely chopped (deseeded if you don't like it too hot)
- 200g tomatoes , roughly chopped
- 50g dried split red lentils , rinsed
- 1/2 small pack of coriander , roughly chopped, plus extra to garnish
- 100g pack baby leaf spinach

For the broccoli rice

- 100g wholegrain brown rice
- 100g small broccoli florets

Method

STEP 1

Put the lamb in a large bowl and season well with ground black pepper. Add the yogurt and 1/ 2 tbsp of the curry powder, and stir well to combine.

STEP 2

Heat half the oil in a large non-stick saucepan. Fry the onion wedges over a high heat for 4-5 mins or until lightly browned and just tender. Tip onto a plate, set aside and return the pan to the heat.

STEP 3

Add the remaining oil, the sliced onions, garlic, ginger and chilli, cover and cook for 10 mins or until very soft, stirring occasionally. Remove the lid, increase the heat and cook for 2-3 mins more or until the onions are tinged with brown – this will add lots of flavour, but make sure they don't get burnt.

STEP 4

Reduce the heat once more and stir in the tomatoes and remaining curry powder. Cook for 1 min, then stir the lamb and yogurt into the pan and cook over a medium-high heat for 4-5 mins, stirring regularly.

STEP 5

Pour 300ml cold water into the pan, stir in the lentils and coriander, cover with a lid and leave to cook over a low heat for 45 mins – the sauce should be simmering gently and you can add a splash of water if the curry gets a little dry. Remove the lid every 10-15 mins and stir the curry.

STEP 6

With half an hour of the curry cooking time remaining, cook the rice in plenty of boiling water for 25 mins or until just tender. Add the broccoli florets and cook for a further 3 mins. Drain well.

STEP 7

Remove the lid from the curry, add the reserved onion wedges and continue to simmer over a high heat for a further 15 mins or until the lamb is tender, stirring regularly. Just before serving, stir in the spinach, a handful at a time, and let it wilt. Serve with the yogurt, coriander and broccoli rice.

Chargrilled chicken & kale Caesar salad

Prep: 20 mins **Cook:** 20 mins

Serves 4

Ingredients

- 1 anchovy
- 1 garlic clove

- 1 tsp Dijon mustard
- 100ml buttermilk
- 1 lemon , zested and juiced
- 200g bag kale , large tough stalks removed
- 200g defrosted frozen peas
- 6 skinless and boneless chicken thighs
- 2 thick slices crusty bread
- 3 tbsp cold pressed rapeseed oil
- 400g long-stem broccoli , cut in half lengthways
- 30g parmesan

Method

STEP 1

Mash the anchovy and garlic together using a pestle and mortar, then tip the mixture into a bowl and whisk in the mustard, buttermilk, lemon zest and juice, and season with black pepper. Put the kale and peas in a large bowl, pour over ¾ of the dressing, then massage into the kale so each leaf is coated.

STEP 2

Put the chicken thighs between two pieces of baking parchment, then bash out with a rolling pin to 1cm thickness.

STEP 3

Heat a griddle pan until searing hot. Brush the bread slices with a little oil, then griddle until lightly charred on all sides. Set aside.

STEP 4

Next, season the broccoli and brush the cut side of each piece with a little oil. Griddle, cut-side down, in batches for 3-4 mins until tender. Lastly, brush the remaining oil over the chicken thighs and season, then griddle the chicken for 3-4 mins on each side until cooked through.

STEP 5

Distribute the kale between four plates. Slice the chicken diagonally and break the bread into pieces. Top each of the plates with ¼ of the chicken, broccoli and croutons. Grate over the parmesan in large shavings and drizzle with the remaining dressing to serve.

Slow cooker Turkish breakfast eggs

Prep: 15 mins **Cook:** 5 hrs - 6 hrs

Serves 4

Ingredients

- 1 tbsp olive oil
- 2 onions , finely sliced
- 1 red pepper , cored and finely sliced
- 1 small red chilli , finely sliced
- 8 cherry tomatoes
- 1 slice sourdough bread , cubed
- 4 eggs
- 2 tbsp skimmed milk
- small bunch parsley , finely chopped
- 4 tbsp natural yogurt , to serve

Method

STEP 1

Oil the inside of a small slow cooker and heat if necessary. Heat the remaining oil in a heavy-based frying pan. Stir in the onions, pepper and chilli. Cook until they begin to soften. Tip into the slow cooker and add the cherry tomatoes and bread and stir everything. Season.

STEP 2

Whisk the eggs with the milk and parsley and pour this over the top, making sure all the other ingredients are covered. Cook for 5-6 hours. Serve with the yogurt.

Prawn fried rice

Prep: 5 mins **Cook:** 25 mins

Serves 4

Ingredients

- 250g long-grain brown rice

- 150g frozen peas
- 100g mangetout
- 1½ tbsp rapeseed oil
- 1 onion , finely chopped
- 2 garlic cloves , crushed
- thumb-sized piece of ginger , finely grated
- 150g raw king prawns
- 3 medium eggs , beaten
- 2 tsp sesame seeds
- 1 tbsp low-salt soy sauce
- ½ tbsp rice or white wine vinegar
- 4 spring onions , trimmed and sliced

Method

STEP 1

Cook the rice following pack instructions. Boil a separate pan of water and blanch the peas and mangetout for 1 min, then drain and set aside with the rice.

STEP 2

Meanwhile, heat the oil in a large non-stick frying pan or wok over a medium heat and fry the onion for 10 mins or until golden brown. Add the garlic and ginger and fry for a further minute. Tip in the blanched vegetables and fry for 5 mins, then the prawns and fry for a further 2 mins. Stir the rice into the pan then push everything to one side. Pour the beaten eggs into the empty side of the pan and stir to scramble them. Fold everything together with the sesame seeds, soy and vinegar, then finish with the spring onions scattered over.

Avocado & bean triangles

Prep:5 mins No cook

Serves 2

Ingredients

- 3 triangluar bread thins
- 210g can red kidney beans , drained
- 1 tbsp finely chopped dill , plus extra for garnish

- 1/2 lemon , for squeezing
- 1 tomato , chopped
- 1 small avocado
- 1 small red onion , finely chopped

Method

STEP 1

Follow our triangular bread thins recipe to make your own. While they bake, roughly mash the beans with the dill and a good squeeze of lemon then stir in the tomato.

STEP 2

Cut the bread triangles in half and top with the beans. Scoop the avocado into a bowl and roughly mash with a squeeze more lemon. Spoon the avocado onto the beans, scatter over the chopped onion, then garnish with the remaining dill.

Ham & piccalilli salad

Prep:15 mins No cook

Serves 4

Ingredients

- 4 tbsp piccalilli
- 3 tbsp natural yogurt
- 12 silverskin pickled onions , halved
- 130g pea shoots
- 180g pulled ham hock or shredded cooked ham
- ½ cucumber , halved and thickly sliced
- 100g fresh peas
- 40g mature cheddar , shaved
- crusty bread , to serve

Method

STEP 1

Mix the piccalilli, yogurt, onions and 4 tbsp water together to make a dressing. Season and set aside.

STEP 2

Toss the pea shoots, ham, cucumber and peas together. Pile onto a serving plate, then drizzle over the dressing. Top with the cheese and serve with crusty bread.

Summer carrot, tarragon & white bean soup

Prep:10 mins **Cook:**20 mins

Serves 4

Ingredients

- 1 tbsp rapeseed oil
- 2 large leeks , well washed, halved lengthways and finely sliced
- 700g carrots , chopped
- 1.4l hot reduced-salt vegetable bouillon (we used Marigold)
- 4 garlic cloves , finely grated
- 2 x 400g cans cannellini beans in water
- ⅔ small pack tarragon , leaves roughly chopped

Method

STEP 1

Heat the oil over a medium heat in a large pan and fry the leeks and carrots for 5 mins to soften.

STEP 2

Pour over the stock, stir in the garlic, the beans with their liquid, and three-quarters of the tarragon, then cover and simmer for 15 mins or until the veg is just tender. Stir in the remaining tarragon before serving.

White velvet soup with smoky almonds

Cook:25 mins **Serves 2**

Ingredients

- 2 tsp rapeseed oil
- 2 large garlic cloves , sliced
- 2 leeks , trimmed so they're mostly white in colour, washed well, then sliced (about 240g)
- 200g cauliflower , chopped
- 2 tsp vegetable bouillon powder
- 400g cannellini beans , rinsed
- fresh nutmeg , for grating
- 100ml whole milk
- 25g whole almonds , chopped
- ½ tsp smoked paprika
- 2 x 25g slices rye bread , to serve

Method

STEP 1

Heat the oil in a large pan. Add the garlic, leeks and cauliflower and cook for about 5 mins, stirring frequently, until starting to soften (but not colouring).

STEP 2

Stir in the vegetable bouillon and beans, pour in 600ml boiling water and add a few generous gratings of the nutmeg. Cover and leave to simmer for 15 mins until the leeks and cauliflower are tender. Add the milk and blitz with a hand blender until smooth and creamy.

STEP 3

Put the almonds in a dry pan and cook very gently for 1 min, or until toasted, then remove from the heat. Scatter the paprika over the almonds and mix well. Ladle the soup into bowls, top with the spicy nuts and serve with the rye bread.

Vegan bolognese

Prep: 20 mins **Cook:** 1 hr

Serves 3

Ingredients

- 15g dried porcini mushrooms
- 1 ½ tbsp olive oil

183

- ½ onion, finely chopped
- 1 carrot, finely chopped
- 1 celery stick, finely chopped
- 2 garlic cloves, sliced
- 2 thyme sprigs
- ½ tsp tomato purée
- 50ml vegan red wine (optional)
- 125g dried green lentils
- 400g can whole plum tomatoes
- 125g chestnut mushrooms, chopped
- 125g portobello mushrooms, sliced
- ½ tsp soy sauce
- ½ tsp Marmite
- 270g spaghetti
- handful fresh basil leaves

Method

STEP 1

Pour 400ml boiling water over the dried porcini and leave for 10 mins until hydrated. Meanwhile pour 1 tbsp oil into a large saucepan. Add the onion, carrot, celery and a pinch of salt. Cook gently, stirring for 10 mins until soft. Remove the porcini from the liquid, keeping the mushroomy stock and roughly chop. Set both aside.

STEP 2

Add the garlic and thyme to the pan. Cook for 1 min then stir in the tomato purée and cook for a min more. Pour in the red wine, if using, cook until nearly reduced, then add the lentils, reserved mushroom stock and tomatoes. Bring to the boil, then reduce the heat and leave to simmer with a lid on.

STEP 3

Meanwhile, heat a large frying pan. Add the remaining oil, then tip in the chestnut, portobello and rehydrated mushrooms. Fry until all the water has evaporated and the mushrooms are deep golden brown. Pour in the soy sauce. Give everything a good mix, then scrape the mushrooms into the lentil mixture.

STEP 4

Stir in the Marmite and continue to cook the ragu, stirring occasionally, over a low-medium heat for 30-45 mins until the lentils are cooked and the sauce is thick and reduced, adding extra water if necessary. Remove the thyme sprigs and season to taste.

STEP 5

Cook the spaghetti in a large pan of salted water for 1 min less than packet instructions. Drain the pasta, reserving a ladleful of pasta water, then toss the spaghetti in the sauce, using a little of the starchy liquid to loosen up the ragu slightly so that the pasta clings to the sauce. Serve topped with fresh basil and some black pepper.

Avocado & strawberry smoothie

Prep:5 mins No cook

Serves 2

Ingredients

- ½ avocado , stoned, peeled and cut into chunks
- 150g strawberry , halved
- 4 tbsp low-fat natural yogurt
- 200ml semi-skimmed milk
- lemon or lime juice , to taste
- honey , to taste

Method

STEP 1

Put all the ingredients in a blender and whizz until smooth. If the consistency is too thick, add a little water.

Samosa pie

Prep:5 mins **Cook:**30 mins

Serves 4

Ingredients

- 2-3 tbsp vegetable oil
- 1 onion , chopped
- 500g lamb mince
- 2 garlic cloves , finely chopped
- 2 tbsp curry powder
- 1 large sweet potato (about 300g), peeled and grated
- 100g frozen peas
- handful coriander , roughly chopped
- juice 0.5 lemon
- 3-4 sheets filo pastry
- 1 tsp cumin seeds

Method

STEP 1

Heat oven to 180C/160C fan/gas 4. Heat 1 tbsp of the oil in a frying pan. Cook the onion and mince for about 5 mins until the meat is browned. Stir in the garlic, curry powder, sweet potato and 300ml water. Cook for 5-8 mins until the potato has softened. Stir in the peas, coriander and a squeeze of lemon juice, then season.

STEP 2

Spoon the mixture into a baking dish. Brush the sheets of filo with the remaining oil and scrunch over the top of the mince. Sprinkle with cumin seeds and bake for 10-15 mins or until the top is crisp.

Red pepper & bean tikka masala

Prep:10 mins **Cook:**20 mins

Serves 2

Ingredients

- 1 tbsp vegetable oil
- 1 onion , chopped
- 2 red peppers , deseeded and cut into strips
- 1 garlic clove , crushed
- thumb-sized piece of ginger , grated

- 1 red chilli , finely chopped
- ½ tbsp garam masala
- ½ tbsp curry powder
- 1 tbsp tomato purée
- 415g can baked beans
- ½ lemon , juiced
- rice and coriander, to serve

Method

STEP 1

Heat the oil in a saucepan over a medium heat, add the onion and red peppers with a pinch of salt and fry until softened, around 5 mins. Tip in the garlic, ginger and red chilli along with the spices and fry for a couple of mins longer.

STEP 2

Spoon in the tomato purée, stir, then tip in the baked beans along with 100ml water. Bubble for 5 mins, then squeeze in the lemon juice. Serve with the rice and scatter over the coriander leaves.

Lentil & cauliflower curry

Prep:10 mins **Cook:**40 mins

Serves 4

Ingredients

- 1 tbsp olive oil
- 1 large onion, chopped
- 3 tbsp curry paste
- 1 tsp turmeric
- 1 tsp mustard seeds
- 200g red or yellow lentil
- 1l low-sodium vegetable or chicken stock (made with 2 cubes)
- 1 large cauliflower, broken into florets
- 1 large potato, diced

- 3 tbsp coconut yogurt
- small pack coriander, chopped
- juice 1 lemon
- 100g cooked brown rice

Method

STEP 1

Heat the oil in a large saucepan and cook the onion until soft, about 5 mins. Add the curry paste, spices and lentils, then stir to coat the lentils in the onions and paste. Pour over the stock and simmer for 20 mins, then add the cauliflower, potato and a little extra water if it looks a bit dry.

STEP 2

Simmer for about 12 mins until the cauliflower and potatoes are tender. Stir in the yogurt, coriander and lemon juice, and serve with the brown rice.

Herby chicken gyros

Prep: 10 mins **Cook:** 4 mins

Serves 2

Ingredients

- 1 large skinless chicken breast
- rapeseed oil , for brushing
- small garlic clove , crushed
- ½ tsp dried oregano
- 2 tbsp Greek yogurt
- 10 cm piece cucumber , grated, excess juice squeezed out
- 2 tbsp chopped mint , plus a few leaves to serve
- 2 wholemeal pitta breads
- 2 red or yellow tomatoes , sliced
- 1 red pepper from a jar (not in oil), deseeded and sliced

Method

STEP 1

Cut the chicken breast in half lengthways, then cover with cling film and bash with a rolling pin to flatten it. Brush with some oil, then cover with the garlic, oregano and some pepper. Heat a non-stick frying pan and cook the chicken for a few mins each side. Meanwhile, mix the yogurt, cucumber and mint to make tzatziki.

STEP 2

Cut the tops from the pittas along their longest side and stuff with the chicken, tomato, pepper and tzatziki. Poke in a few mint leaves to serve. If taking to the office for lunch, pack the tzatziki in a separate pot and add just before eating to prevent the pitta going soggy before lunchtime.

Spicy chicken & bean stew

Prep: 15 mins **Cook:** 1 hr and 20 mins

Serves 6

Ingredients

- 1¼ kg chicken thighs and drumsticks (approx. weight, we used a 1.23kg mixed pack)
- 1 tbsp olive oil
- 2 onions, sliced
- 1 garlic clove, crushed
- 2 red chillies, deseeded and chopped
- 250g frozen peppers, defrosted
- 400g can chopped tomatoes
- 420g can kidney beans in chilli sauce
- 2 x 400g cans butter beans, drained
- 400ml hot chicken stock
- small bunch coriander, chopped
- 150ml pot soured cream and crusty bread, to serve

Method

STEP 1

Pull the skin off the chicken and discard. Heat the oil in a large casserole dish, brown the chicken all over, then remove with a slotted spoon. Tip in the onions, garlic and chillies, then fry for 5 mins until starting to soften and turn golden.

STEP 2

Add the peppers, tomatoes, beans and hot stock. Put the chicken back on top, half-cover with a pan lid and cook for 50 mins, until the chicken is cooked through and tender.

STEP 3

Stir through the coriander and serve with soured cream and crusty bread.

Spice-crusted aubergines & peppers with pilaf

Prep:10 mins **Cook:**30 mins

Serves 4

Ingredients

- 2 large aubergines , halved
- 2 tbsp extra virgin olive oil
- 2 red peppers , quartered
- 2 tsp ground cinnamon
- 2 tsp chilli flakes
- 2 tsp za'atar
- 4 tbsp pomegranate molasses
- 140g puy lentils
- 140g basmati rice
- seeds from 1 pomegranate
- small pack flat-leaf parsley , roughly chopped
- Greek or coconut yogurt , to serve

Method

STEP 1

Heat oven to 220C/200C fan/gas 7. Using a sharp knife, score a diamond pattern into the aubergines. Brush with 1 tbsp of the oil, season well and place on a baking tray, cut-side down. Cook in the oven for 15 mins. Add the peppers to the tray, turn the aubergines over and drizzle everything with the remaining oil. Sprinkle over the spices, 1 tbsp of the pomegranate molasses and a little salt. Roast in the oven for 15 mins more.

STEP 2

Boil the lentils in plenty of water until al dente. After they've been boiling for 5 mins, add the rice. Cook for 10 mins or until cooked through but with a bit of bite. Drain and return to the pan, covered with a lid to keep warm.

STEP 3

Stir the pomegranate seeds and parsley through the lentil rice. Divide between four plates or tip onto a large platter. Top with the roasted veg, a dollop of yogurt and the remaining pomegranate molasses drizzled over.

Potato pancakes with chard & eggs

Prep: 10 mins **Cook:** 15 mins

Serves 2

Ingredients

- 300g mashed potato
- 4 spring onions , very finely chopped
- 25g plain wholemeal flour
- ½ tsp baking powder
- 3 eggs
- 2 tsp rapeseed oil
- 240g chard , stalks and leaves roughly chopped, or baby spinach, chopped

Method

STEP 1

Mix the mash, spring onions, flour, baking powder and 1 of the eggs in a bowl. Heat the oil in a non-stick frying pan, then spoon in the potato mix to make two mounds. Flatten them to form two 15cm discs and fry for 5-8 mins until the undersides are set and golden, then carefully ip over and cook on the other side.

STEP 2

Meanwhile, wash the chard and put in a pan with some of the water still clinging to it, then cover and cook over a medium heat for 5 mins until wilted and tender. Poach the remaining eggs.

STEP 3

Top the pancakes with the greens and egg. Serve while the yolks are still runny.

Sunshine smoothie

Prep: 5 mins no cook

Serves 3

Ingredients

- 500ml carrot juice, chilled
- 200g pineapple (fresh or canned)
- 2 bananas, broken into chunks
- small piece ginger, peeled
- 20g cashew nuts
- juice 1 lime

Method

STEP 1

Put the ingredients in a blender and whizz until smooth. Drink straight away or pour into a bottle to drink on the go. Will keep in the fridge for a day.

Crispy cod fingers with wedges & dill slaw

Prep: 30 mins **Cook:** 40 mins

Serves 4

Ingredients

- 3 large sweet potatoes (700g), scrubbed and cut into wedges
- ½ tbsp sunflower oil , plus a little extra
- ¼ large red cabbage

- ½ medium red onion , finely sliced
- 6 large cornichons , quartered
- 3 tbsp Greek yogurt or mayonnaise
- 25g dill , finely chopped
- 4 skinned cod fillets (160g per fillet)
- 2 large eggs
- 100g fresh breadcrumbs

Method

STEP 1

Heat oven to 200C/180C fan/gas 6. In a bowl, toss the wedges with the oil, 1 tsp salt and 1/4 tsp pepper. Transfer to a baking sheet and roast for 25-30 mins, turning halfway through. The wedges should be crisp and golden brown.

STEP 2

Meanwhile, make the slaw. Remove the cabbage's white core and discard. Slice the leaves as finely as possible and put in a large mixing bowl with the onion and cornichons. In another bowl, combine the yogurt or mayonnaise with the dill and 2 tbsp of the cornichons' pickling liquid. Mix the dressing with the other slaw ingredients until everything is well coated, then set aside.

STEP 3

Heat grill to high. Slice each cod fillet into two or three fingers. Beat the eggs lightly in a shallow bowl and tip the breadcrumbs into a separate bowl with a good pinch of salt and pepper. Dip each cod finger in the egg and then in the breadcrumbs, and place on an oiled baking sheet. Grill for 6-7 mins or until cooked through and golden. Serve with the crispy wedges and a generous helping of the dill pickle slaw.

Falafel burgers

Prep:10 mins **Cook:**6 mins

Serves 4

Ingredients

- 400g can chickpeas, rinsed and drained

- 1 small red onion, roughly chopped
- 1 garlic clove, chopped
- handful of flat-leaf parsley or curly parsley
- 1 tsp ground cumin
- 1 tsp ground coriander
- ½ tsp harissa paste or chilli powder
- 2 tbsp plain flour
- 2 tbsp sunflower oil
- toasted pitta bread, to serve
- 200g tub tomato salsa, to serve
- green salad, to serve

Method

STEP 1

Drain the chickpeas and pat dry with kitchen paper. Tip into a food processor along with the onion, garlic, parsley, cumin, coriander, harissa paste, flour and a little salt. Blend until fairly smooth, then shape into four patties with your hands.

STEP 2

Heat the sunflower oil in a non-stick frying pan, and fry the burgers for 3 mins on each side until lightly golden. Serve with the toasted pitta bread, tomato salsa and green salad.

Buckwheat with charred baby aubergines

Prep:15 mins **Cook:**20 mins

Serves 4

Ingredients

- 350g baby aubergines , halved
- 8 whole spring onions , tops trimmed
- 250g buckwheat
- 2 tbsp cold pressed rapeseed oil
- 1 x 400g can green lentils , drained
- 30g dried cherries , roughly chopped

- 8 walnut halves, finely chopped
- 1 lemon , juiced
- ½ tsp chilli flakes
- small bunch dill , finely chopped
- 30g soft goat's cheese , crumbled

Method

STEP 1

Heat the grill to its highest setting. Spread the aubergines out on a baking sheet, cut-side up, and grill for 10-15 mins until they begin to soften and blister.

STEP 2

Meanwhile, heat a griddle pan over a high heat. Add the spring onions and cook on each side for 5-6 mins until softened and charred. Remove with tongs and set aside.

STEP 3

Bring a medium-sized pan of water to the boil. Tip the buckwheat into a frying pan and dry fry over a medium heat for 3 mins until lightly toasted. Add the buckwheat to the boiling water and cook for 4-5 mins. Drain and toss with the oil. Leave to cool down for 5 mins.

STEP 4

Toss the warm buckwheat, lentils, cherries, walnuts, lemon juice, chilli and most of the dill in a bowl. Spread out on a serving plate and top with the aubergines, charred spring onions, remaining dill and goat's cheese.

Steamed salmon & veg rice bowl

Prep: 10 mins **Cook:** 15 mins - 20 mins

Serves 4

Ingredients

- 200g brown rice
- 100g green beans
- 200g pak choi , chopped into chunky pieces
- 4 x 100g salmon fillets

- For the dressing
- 4 tbsp kecap manis (sweet soy sauce)
- juice 3 limes
- 2 tbsp sambal oelek (chopped chilli in a jar) or 1 red chilli, deseeded and chopped
- 1 tbsp rice vinegar
- 1 tbsp golden caster sugar
- To serve
- 4 spring onions , finely chopped
- 4 tbsp mixed seeds (I used pumpkin, sesame and sunflower)
- pickled ginger , chopped (optional)

Method

STEP 1

In a small bowl, mix together the dressing ingredients, then set aside. Boil the rice in plenty of water and drain when just cooked, about 15 mins.

STEP 2

Meanwhile, put the vegetables and fish in a large steamer in two layers. Steam the fish for 5-8 mins and the veg for 4-5 mins until cooked through. Spoon the rice into bowls and top with the steamed fish and veg. Pour some dressing over and top with the spring onions, mixed seeds and pickled ginger, if you like.

Caramelised onion & goat's cheese pizza

Prep:20 mins **Cook:**30 mins

Serves 2

Ingredients

For the base

- 125g wholemeal flour , plus a little for kneading if necessary
- ½ tsp instant yeast
- pinch of salt
- 1 tsp rapeseed oil , plus extra for greasing

For the topping

- 2 onions , halved and thinly sliced
- 2 tsp rapeseed oil
- 2 tsp balsamic vinegar
- 160g baby spinach leaves (not the very tiny ones), chopped
- 2 large garlic cloves , finely grated
- 50g soft goat's cheese
- 4 pitted Kalamata olives , quartered
- few soft thyme leaves
- 1 tsp sunflower seeds

Method

STEP 1

Heat oven to 220C/200C fan/gas 7. Tip the flour into a mixer with a dough hook, or a bowl. Add the yeast, salt, oil and just under 100ml warm water then mix to a soft dough. Knead in the food mixer for about 5 mins, but if making this by hand, tip onto a work surface and knead for about 10 mins. The dough is sticky, but try not to add too much extra flour. Leave in the bowl and cover with a tea towel while you make the topping. There is no need to let the dough prove for a specific time – just let it sit while you get on with the next step.

STEP 2

Tip the onions into a non-stick wok and add the oil, 4 tbsp water and balsamic vinegar. Cover with a saucepan lid that sits inside the pan to help the onions soften, then cook for 15 mins, stirring about 3 times and replacing the lid quickly so as not to lose too much moisture. After the time is up, the onions should be golden and all the liquid gone. Tip onto a plate. Add the spinach and garlic to the pan and stir-fry until the spinach has wilted.

STEP 3

Take the dough from the bowl and cut in half with an oiled knife, then press each piece into a 25-15 cm oval on a large greased baking sheet with oiled hands. Don't knead the dough first otherwise it will be too elastic and it will keep shrinking back.

STEP 4

Spread with the spinach followed by the onions, then dot with the cheese and scatter with the olives, thyme and sunflower seeds. Bake for 15 mins until golden and the base is cooked through.

Chilli tempeh stir-fry

Prep: 10 mins **Cook:** 15 mins

Serves 2

Ingredients

- 300g long-stem broccoli
- ½ tbsp toasted sesame oil
- 150g tempeh , sliced and cut into 2cm cubes
- 2 garlic cloves , thinly sliced
- 1 thumb-sized piece ginger , peeled and finely grated
- ½ small red chilli , deseeded and finely chopped
- ½ tbsp gochujang paste
- 1 tsp sesame seeds
- steamed brown rice , to serve (optional)

Method

STEP 1

Boil the broccoli for 1 min 30 secs. Drain.

STEP 2

Heat the oil in a non-stick pan. Stir-fry the tempeh for 2-3 mins, then put on a plate. Fry the garlic, ginger and chilli for 2 mins. Tip in the broccoli and toss.

STEP 3

Mix the gochujang with 2 tbsp water and the tempeh. Add to the pan with the seeds. Cook for 2 mins. Serve with rice, if you like.

Chive waffles with maple & soy mushrooms

Prep: 25 mins **Cook:** 20 mins

Serves 6

Ingredients

- 500ml soya milk or rice milk
- 1 tsp cider vinegar or lemon juice
- 2 tbsp rapeseed oil
- 100g cooked, mashed sweet potato
- 150g polenta
- 130g plain flour
- 1 tbsp baking powder
- small bunch chives , snipped
- 1 tbsp maple syrup
- 2 tsp light soy sauce
- 6 large mushrooms , thickly sliced
- olive oil , for frying
- soya yogurt , to serve (optional)

Method

STEP 1

Heat the waffle iron. Mix the soya or rice milk with the vinegar and rapeseed oil (don't worry if it starts to split), then whisk in the sweet potato mash. Tip the polenta, flour and baking powder into a bowl, mix and make a well in the centre. Add a large pinch of salt, then slowly pour in the milk mixture and whisk to make a batter. Stir in half the chives.

STEP 2

Pour enough batter into the waffle iron to fill and cook for 4-5 mins. Lift out the waffle, keep it warm and repeat with the remaining mixture until you have six waffles.

STEP 3

Meanwhile, mix the maple syrup with the soy sauce. Brush it over the mushrooms and season with pepper. Heat a little oil in a frying pan and fry the mushrooms on both sides until they are browned and cooked through – make sure they don't burn at the edges. Serve the waffles topped with mushrooms, add a spoonful of soya yogurt, if you like, and scatter over the remaining chives.

South Indian coconut & prawn curry

Prep:15 mins **Cook:**25 mins - 30 mins

Serves 2

Ingredients

- 1 large onion , quartered
- 0.5 thumb-sized piece ginger (no need to peel)
- 4 garlic cloves
- 4 tomatoes , 2 halved, 2 cut into wedges
- 2 tsp rapeseed oil
- ½ cinnamon stick
- ½ tsp black mustard seeds
- 3 cloves
- seeds from 4 cardamom pods , crushed
- ½ tsp ground turmeric
- 1 tsp ground coriander
- 10 fresh or dried curry leaves
- ½ fish stock cube
- 15g creamed coconut , chopped
- 1 red chilli , halved, deseeded and sliced or diced
- 150g pack raw, shelled king prawns
- 140g skinless cod , cut in half, then halve again to make chunky strips

Method

STEP 1

Put the onion, ginger, garlic and the halved tomatoes in a food processor with 50ml water and blitz to a smooth purée. You may need to scrape down the inside of the food processor a couple of times. Heat the oil in a large, deep non-stick frying pan, pour in the purée, cover with a lid and cook for 10 mins.

STEP 2

Add the 1/2 cinnamon stick, mustard seeds, cloves, cardamom, turmeric, coriander and curry leaves, and cook for a few mins, stirring. Pour in 300ml water with the stock cube, coconut and chilli, then leave to simmer for 10 mins more. Taste to ensure that the onion is fully cooked – if not, it is worth cooking for another 5 mins.

STEP 3

Finally, add the tomato wedges, prawns and fish, gently stir into the sauce, then cover and cook for 5 mins. Serve with the Spicy cauliflower pilau (see Goes well with).

Harissa trout, beetroot & grapefruit salad with whipped feta

Prep:20 mins **Cook:**45 mins

Serves 2

Ingredients

- 300g raw beetroot , scrubbed, skin left on
- 30g feta
- 2 tbsp 0% fat natural yogurt
- 1 lemon , zested and juiced
- 2 tbsp quinoa (optional)
- 1 pink grapefruit
- 1 tbsp extra virgin olive oil
- 1 tbsp harissa
- 2 trout fillets
- 2 red chicory , separated into leaves
- ½ small pack dill , leaves picked

Method

STEP 1

Bring a saucepan of water to the boil. Season the water, drop in the beetroot and cover the pan with a lid. Cook for 30-45 mins, depending on their size, until a cutlery knife can be easily inserted into them.

STEP 2

Meanwhile, heat oven to 200C/180C fan/gas 6. Put the feta in a bowl and mash with a fork, then beat in the yogurt and season with the lemon juice and zest to taste. In a dry frying pan, toast the quinoa, if using, until it pops. Set both aside.

STEP 3

Segment the grapefruit over a bowl to catch the juices, squeezing out as much as possible. Put the segments to one side, then whisk the olive oil with the juice. Season to taste with lemon juice, salt and pepper. You want it to be really tangy, as all the acidity will be absorbed by the beets.

STEP 4

Rub the harissa over the trout, season, then roast in the oven for 8-10 mins until just cooked.

STEP 5

Drain the beetroot. Once cool enough to handle, peel off the skin – it should come away easily. Cut into segments, then put onto a salad plate along with the chicory leaves. Pour the dressing over the warm beets and toss together. Nestle in the grapefruit segments, trout, harissa and dill, then add dollops of the feta and scatter over the toasted quinoa, if using.

Squash & lentil salad

Prep:10 mins **Cook:**35 mins

Serves 2

Ingredients

- 350g chopped butternut squash
- 4 tbsp olive oil
- 75g cucumber & mint raita or tzatziki
- 250g pack puy lentils
- small bunch dill

Method

STEP 1

Heat oven to 220C/200C/gas 7. Toss the squash in 2 tbsp olive oil, season and roast for 30-35 mins or until golden.

STEP 2

Add 2-3 tsp water to the raita, stir until smooth and set aside. Toss the lentils with half the raita, squash and dill. Tip the lentils onto a plate, top with remaining squash, drizzle over 2 tsp olive oil and the rest of the raita. Garnish with the remaining dill.

Kale & bulgur tabbouleh with yogurt dressing

Prep:15 mins **Cook:**15 mins

Serves 2

Ingredients

- 150g bulgur wheat
- 2 eggs
- 60g baby kale or curly kale, roughly chopped
- 20g hazelnuts , toasted and roughly chopped
- 1 carrot , julienned
- 3 spring onions , roughly chopped
- 50g pomegranate seeds
- 1 tsp chilli flakes
- juice 1 lemon

For the dressing

- 100ml 0% fat Greek yoghurt
- juice and zest 1 lemon
- 2 tbsp white wine vinegar
- 1 tbsp chopped dill
- 1 tbsp chopped mint
- ¼ garlic clove , crushed

Method

STEP 1

Put the bulgur in a medium bowl and pour over 125ml boiling water. Mix well, cover the bowl with cling film and leave for 10-15 mins until al dente.

STEP 2

Bring a pan of water to the boil and add the eggs. Cook for 6 mins, then place in cold water until cool. Peel and cut in half. Put the dressing ingredients in a food processor or blender with 2 tbsp water and some salt. Blend until smooth.

STEP 3

Break up the bulgur with a fork and add the remaining ingredients, except the eggs. Toss with the dressing, then top with the eggs to serve.

Sweet potato & sprout hash with poached eggs

Prep:15 mins **Cook:**25 mins

Serves 3

Ingredients

- 2 large sweet potatoes , cut into chunks
- 2 tsp olive oil
- 2 red onions , thinly sliced
- 300g Brussels sprouts , thinly sliced
- grating of nutmeg
- 3 eggs

Method

STEP 1

Put the sweet potatoes in a bowl, cover with cling film and microwave on high for 5 mins until tender but still holding their shape. Uncover the bowl and leave to cool a little.

STEP 2

Meanwhile, heat the oil in a wide non-stick frying pan and add the onions. Cook for 5-8 mins until starting to caramelise. Add the sprouts and stir-fry over a high heat until softened. Push the sprouts and onions to one side of the pan and add the sweet potatoes, squashing them down in the pan with the back of a spatula. Leave undisturbed for 5 mins until starting to crisp on the underside. Season, add the nutmeg, mix in the sprouts and onions, and flip the potato over, trying not to break it up too much. Cook for a further 5 mins until really crispy.

STEP 3

Meanwhile, poach 3 eggs in a pan of barely simmering water. Serve the hash topped with poached eggs.

Prawn jalfrezi

Prep:10 mins **Cook:**22 mins

Serves 2

Ingredients

- 2 tsp rapeseed oil
- 2 medium onions , chopped
- thumb-sized piece ginger , finely chopped
- 2 garlic cloves , chopped
- 1 tsp ground coriander
- ½ tsp ground turmeric
- ½ tsp ground cumin
- ¼ tsp chilli flakes (or less if you don't like it too spicy)
- 400g can chopped tomato
- squeeze of clear honey
- 1 large green pepper , halved, deseeded and chopped
- small bunch coriander , stalks and leaves separated, chopped
- 140g large cooked peeled tiger prawns
- 250g pouch cooked brown rice
- minty yogurt or chutney, to serve (optional)

Method

STEP 1

Heat the oil in a non-stick pan and fry the onions, ginger and garlic for 8-10 mins, stirring frequently, until softened and starting to colour. Add the spices and chilli flakes, stir briefly, then pour in the tomatoes with half a can of water and the honey. Blitz everything in the pan with a hand blender until almost smooth (or use a food processor). Stir in the pepper and coriander stalks, cover the pan and leave to simmer for 10 mins. (The mixture will be very thick and splutter a little, so stir frequently.)

STEP 2

Stir in the prawns and scatter over the coriander leaves. Heat the rice following pack instructions. Serve both with a minty yogurt or chutney, if you like.

Vegan chocolate banana ice cream

Prep:5 mins **Serves 1**

Ingredients

- 1 frozen banana
- 1 tsp cocoa powder

Method

STEP 1

In a blender, blitz the frozen banana with the cocoa powder until smooth. Eat straight away.

Baked cod with goat's cheese & thyme

Prep:10 mins **Cook:**12 mins

Serves 2

Ingredients

- 1 tsp rapeseed oil
- 1 garlic clove , grated
- 200g spinach
- 2 x 125g skinless cod fillets
- 25g soft goat's cheese
- 2 tomatoes , each sliced into 3
- a few thyme leaves , to serve

Method

STEP 1

Heat oven to 200C/180C fan/gas 6. Heat the oil in a non-stick pan, add the garlic and fry very briefly to soften it. Tip in the spinach and stir until wilted. Spoon into the base of two gratin dishes, then top with the cod. Spread over some of the goat's cheese and arrange the tomatoes on top.

STEP 2

Snip over a few thyme leaves, then bake for 10 mins until the fish flakes easily when tested. Serve in the dishes.

Cod & smashed celeriac

Prep:10 mins **Cook:**45 mins

Serves 2

Ingredients

- 1 small celeriac , peeled and chopped
- 3 tbsp olive oil
- 1 tsp fennel seeds
- 4 spring onions , each cut into 3 on the diagonal
- 1 courgette , grated
- 1 garlic clove , crushed
- 2 x 125g skinless cod fillets
- 1 lemon , ½ juiced and ½ cut into wedges, to serve
- 1 tbsp chopped parsley leaves, to serve
- rocket leaves , to serve

Method

STEP 1

Heat oven to 200C/180C fan/gas 6. Put the celeriac into a roasting tin, drizzle with 2 tbsp oil, then sprinkle over the fennel seeds. Season and bake in the oven for 45 mins, stirring halfway through, until lightly charred.

STEP 2

While the celeriac cooks, put the spring onions in a dry pan and cook over a high heat for 3-4 mins, turning occasionally, until starting to char. Spread two large sheets of foil out on your work surface. Divide the spring onions between the foil sheets, then top with the grated courgette, garlic and fish. Season and drizzle over the lemon juice and the remaining 1 tbsp olive oil. Scrunch up the edges of the foil to seal and create two parcels. Put the parcels on a baking sheet and bake in the oven for 10-12 mins.

STEP 3

When the celeriac is cooked, mash the pieces with a potato masher or a fork and season well. Pile the smashed celeriac onto plates, then carefully open the fish parcels – the contents will be hot – and gently slide onto the plates next to the celeriac. Garnish with parsley and serve with rocket leaves and lemon wedges.

Lighter South Indian fish curry

Prep:20 mins **Cook:**20 mins

Serves 4

Ingredients

- 1 tbsp rapeseed oil
- ½ tsp cumin seeds
- 1 medium onion , halved lengthways and thinly sliced into wedges
- 3 garlic cloves , finely chopped
- 1 tbsp finely chopped ginger (about a 2.5cm/1in piece)
- 12 dried curry leaves
- 1 tsp black mustard seeds
- 2 small green chillies , halved lengthways, deseeded (or leave a few seeds in if you want a bit of heat)
- 1 tsp ground coriander
- ½ tsp garam masala
- ¼ tsp turmeric
- 400g can reduced-fat coconut milk
- ¼ tsp ground black pepper
- 500g skinned, firm white fish fillets, such as cod or haddock
- 100g fine green beans , trimmed and halved lengthways
- 1 ripe mango
- generous handful roughly chopped coriander , leaves only

- 200g basmati rice , cooked, to serve
- lime wedges, to serve

Method

STEP 1

Heat the oil in a large non-stick frying or sauté pan. Add the cumin seeds and fry for 1 min, then tip in the onion, garlic and ginger, and fry for 1 min more. Stir in the curry leaves and mustard seeds, and fry about 3-4 mins on a medium heat, stirring occasionally, until the onions are turning brown. Stir in the chillies, coriander, garam masala and turmeric, and fry for 30 secs.

STEP 2

Stir the coconut milk in the can, then pour half into the pan. It should start to bubble and thicken, so let it simmer until quite thick, about 3 mins, stirring occasionally. Pour in the rest of the coconut milk, add the pepper and a pinch of salt, and lower the heat.

STEP 3

Sit the fish in the coconut milk and press it down to half submerge it. Cover the pan and simmer gently for 4-5 mins (depending on the thickness of your fillets) until the fish is almost cooked. Do not stir or the fish will break up – just spoon some of the sauce over the top of the fish halfway through, then remove the pan from the heat and let the fish sit for another 3-4 mins to finish cooking slowly. When done, it should feel firm and no longer be opaque. If you want a thinner sauce, pour in a spoonful or two of water.

STEP 4

Meanwhile, steam the green beans for about 4 mins until just tender. De-stone the mango and slice the flesh into thin wedges (see tip below left), then scatter over the fish to warm through.

STEP 5

To serve, break the fish into big chunks by removing it to serving bowls with a slotted spoon, then pour the sauce over and around it. Serve with the beans, a scattering of coriander and the rice, with lime wedges on the side to squeeze over.

Beef goulash soup

Prep:15 mins **Cook:**1 hr

Serves 2 - 3

Ingredients

- 1 tbsp rapeseed oil
- 1 large onion, halved and sliced
- 3 garlic cloves, sliced
- 200g extra lean stewing beef, finely diced
- 1 tsp caraway seeds
- 2 tsp smoked paprika
- 400g can chopped tomatoes
- 600ml beef stock
- 1 medium sweet potato, peeled and diced
- 1 green pepper, deseeded and diced

Supercharged topping

- 150g pot natural bio yogurt
- good handful parsley, chopped

Method

STEP 1

Heat the oil in a large pan, add the onion and garlic, and fry for 5 mins until starting to colour. Stir in the beef, increase the heat and fry, stirring, to brown it.

STEP 2

Add the caraway and paprika, stir well, then tip in the tomatoes and stock. Cover and leave to cook gently for 30 mins.

STEP 3

Stir in the sweet potato and green pepper, cover and cook for 20 mins more or until tender. Allow to cool a little, then serve topped with the yogurt and parsley (if the soup is too hot, it will kill the beneficial bacteria in the yogurt).

Spinach & chickpea curry

Prep:5 mins **Cook:**15 mins

Serves 4

Ingredients

- 2 tbsp mild curry paste
- 1 onion, chopped
- 400g can cherry tomatoes
- 2 x 400g cans chickpeas, drained and rinsed
- 250g bag baby leaf spinach
- squeeze lemon juice
- basmati rice, to serve

Method

STEP 1

Heat the curry paste in a large non-stick frying pan. Once it starts to split, add the onion and cook for 2 mins to soften. Tip in the tomatoes and bubble for 5 mins or until the sauce has reduced.

STEP 2

Add the chickpeas and some seasoning, then cook for 1 min more. Take off the heat, then tip in the spinach and allow the heat of the pan to wilt the leaves. Season, add the lemon juice, and serve with basmati rice.

Creamy sprout, hazelnut & leek pasta

Prep:15 mins **Cook:**25 mins

Serves 4

Ingredients

- ½ tbsp rapeseed oil
- 3 leeks , halved and sliced
- 200g Brussels sprouts , ½ chopped and ½ quartered
- 2 garlic cloves , rushed
- 50ml low-salt vegetable stock
- 3 tbsp low-fat crème fraîche

- 350g short pasta (riciolli or fusilli work well)
- 1 tbsp grated parmesan or veggie alternative
- 1 lemon , zested
- ½ small bunch of parsley , finely chopped
- 1 tbsp chopped hazelnuts , toasted

Method

STEP 1

Heat the oil in a large frying pan over a low heat. Add the leeks and sprouts and cook for 10-15 mins or until softened. Add the garlic and cook for 1 min. Stir through the hot stock and crème fraîche.

STEP 2

Cook the pasta following pack instructions. Drain and toss with the leeks and sprouts, parmesan, lemon, parsley and hazelnuts, adding a ladleful of the pasta cooking water if needed to loosen. Season to taste and spoon into four bowls.

Slow cooker whole chicken

Prep: 15 mins **Cook:** 5 hrs

Serves 6

Ingredients

- 1 large chicken

Method

STEP 1

Heat the slow cooker if necessary and add a splash of water to the base. Scrunch up some foil to make a trivet to sit in the base of the bowl to rest the chicken on. Put the chicken into the pot and season the skin. Cover and cook on Low for 5 hours or until the leg or wing feels very loose when you wiggle it. Tip the juices inside the chicken out as you lift it out.

STEP 2

Brown the chicken skin under the grill or carve the chicken before anyone sees it. Spoon the liquid out of the base of the pan to use as gravy, there won't be much but it will have a good flavour.

Spicy harissa chicken with lentils

Prep:10 mins **Cook:**45 mins

Serves 4

Ingredients

- 1 tbsp olive oil
- 1 red onion , chopped
- 1 garlic clove , crushed
- 50g harissa
- 500g chicken thigh , skin removed, boned and diced
- 1 medium carrot , grated
- 200g dried puy lentils
- 2 x 400g cans chopped tomatoes
- 1.2l stock , made from 1 chicken or vegetable stock cube
- flat-leaf parsley , to serve (optional)

Method

STEP 1

Heat the oil in a large frying pan. Fry the onion on a low heat for 5-6 mins until softened and translucent. Add the garlic and cook for 1 min more.

STEP 2

Stir in the harissa, add the chicken and cook until well browned all over. Stir in the carrot, lentils and tomatoes, then add the stock so the chicken is fully immersed.

STEP 3

Reduce the heat and cook, uncovered, for 30-35 mins until the chicken is thoroughly cooked, and the lentils are tender and have absorbed the liquid. Season well, scatter with parsley (if using) and serve.

Mexican chicken stew

Prep:20 mins **Cook:**25 mins

Serves 4

Ingredients

- 1 tbsp vegetable oil
- 1 medium onion, finely chopped
- 3 garlic cloves, finely chopped
- ½ tsp dark brown sugar
- 1 tsp chipotle paste (we used Discovery)
- 400g can chopped tomatoes
- 4 skinless, boneless chicken breasts
- 1 small red onion, sliced into rings
- a few coriander leaves
- corn tortillas, or rice to serve

Method

STEP 1

Heat the oil in a medium saucepan. Add the onion and cook for 5 mins or until softened and starting to turn golden, adding the garlic for the final min. Stir in the sugar, chipotle paste and tomatoes. Put the chicken into the pan, spoon over the sauce, and simmer gently for 20 mins until the chicken has cooked (add a splash of water if the sauce gets too dry).

STEP 2

Remove the chicken from the pan and shred with 2 forks, then stir back into the sauce. Scatter with a little red onion, the coriander, and serve with remaining red onion, tortillas or rice.

STEP 3

If you want to use a slow cooker, cook the onion and garlic as above, then put into your slow cooker with the sugar, chipotle, tomatoes and chicken. Cover and cook on High for 2 hours. Remove the chicken and shred then serve as above.

Harissa salmon with zesty couscous

Prep: 10 mins **Cook:** 15 mins

Serves 2

Ingredients

- 2 skinless salmon fillets
- zest and juice 1 orange
- 1 tbsp olive oil
- 1-2 tsp rose harissa (depending on how spicy you like it)
- 100g couscous
- ¼ cucumber , finely diced
- 1 small red onion , finely diced
- small pack parsley , chopped, or 1/2 handful mint
- 1 tbsp flaked almond , toasted (optional)

Method

STEP 1

Heat oven to 200C/180C fan/gas 6 and arrange the salmon in a shallow ovenproof dish. Mix the orange juice with the oil and harissa, then pour over the salmon and bake for 10-12 mins until the fish flakes easily, but is still moist.

STEP 2

Meanwhile, put the couscous in a pan with the orange zest, 200ml water and a sprinkling of salt. Heat until the water bubbles round the edges of the pan, then cover and turn off the heat. After 5 mins, tip the couscous into a bowl, add the cucumber, onion, parsley and almonds (if using) and toss together ready to serve with the salmon and spicy juices.

Broccoli and kale green soup

Prep: 15 mins **Cook:** 20 mins

Serves 2

Ingredients

- 500ml stock , made by mixing 1 tbsp bouillon powder and boiling water in a jug
- 1 tbsp sunflower oil

- 2 garlic cloves , sliced
- thumb-sized piece ginger , sliced
- ½ tsp ground coriander
- 3cm/1in piece fresh turmeric root, peeled and grated, or 1/2 tsp ground turmeric
- pinch of pink Himalayan salt
- 200g courgettes , roughly sliced
- 85g broccoli
- 100g kale , chopped
- 1 lime , zested and juiced
- small pack parsley , roughly chopped, reserving a few whole leaves to serve

Method

STEP 1

Put the oil in a deep pan, add the garlic, ginger, coriander, turmeric and salt, fry on a medium heat for 2 mins, then add 3 tbsp water to give a bit more moisture to the spices.

STEP 2

Add the courgettes, making sure you mix well to coat the slices in all the spices, and continue cooking for 3 mins. Add 400ml stock and leave to simmer for 3 mins.

STEP 3

Add the broccoli, kale and lime juice with the rest of the stock. Leave to cook again for another 3-4 mins until all the vegetables are soft.

STEP 4

Take off the heat and add the chopped parsley. Pour everything into a blender and blend on high speed until smooth. It will be a beautiful green with bits of dark speckled through (which is the kale). Garnish with lime zest and parsley.

Healthy banana bread

Prep:20 mins **Cook:**1 hr and 15 mins

Cuts into 10 slices

Ingredients

- low-fat spread, for the tin, plus extra to serve
- 140g wholemeal flour
- 100g self-raising flour
- 1 tsp bicarbonate of soda
- 1 tsp baking powder
- 300g mashed banana from overripe black bananas
- 4 tbsp agave syrup
- 3 large eggs, beaten with a fork
- 150ml pot low-fat natural yogurt
- 25g chopped pecan or walnuts (optional)

Method

STEP 1

Heat oven to 160C/140C fan/gas 3. Grease and line a 2lb loaf tin with baking parchment (allow it to come 2cm above top of tin). Mix the flours, bicarb, baking powder and a pinch of salt in a large bowl.

STEP 2

Mix the bananas, syrup, eggs and yogurt. Quickly stir into dry ingredients, then gently scrape into the tin and scatter with nuts, if using. Bake for 1 hr 10 mins-1 hr 15 mins or until a skewer comes out clean.

STEP 3

Cool in tin on a wire rack. Eat warm or at room temperature, with low-fat spread.

Easy creamy coleslaw

Prep:20 mins No cook

Serves 4

Ingredients

- ½ white cabbage , shredded
- 2 carrots , grated
- 4 spring onions , chopped
- 2 tbsp sultanas

- 3 tbsp low-fat mayonnaise
- 1 tbsp wholegrain mustard

Method

STEP 1

Put the cabbage, carrots, spring onions and sultanas in a large bowl and stir to combine.

STEP 2

Mix the mayonnaise with the mustard in another small bowl and drizzle over the veg. Fold everything together to coat in the creamy sauce, then season to taste.

Teriyaki pork meatballs

Prep:1 min **Cook:**13 mins

Serves 4

Ingredients

- 250g dried medium egg noodles
- 12 fresh pork meatballs
- 300g pak choi
- 6 tbsp teriyaki sauce

Method

STEP 1

Cook the noodles following pack instructions. Add 2 tbsp sunflower oil to a frying pan over a medium heat. Fry the meatballs for 3 mins or until golden brown all over. Lower the heat and cook for 6 mins more. Quarter the pak choi, raise the heat, add the pak choi and cook for 3 mins. Stir through the teriyaki sauce and toss everything together with the drained noodles. Divide between bowls and serve.

Creamy squash linguine

Prep:5 mins **Cook:**1 hr

Serves 4

Ingredients

- 350g chopped butternut squash
- 3 peeled garlic cloves
- 3 tbsp olive oil
- 350g linguine
- small bunch sage

Method

STEP 1

Heat oven to 200C/180C fan/gas 6. Put the squash and garlic on a baking tray and drizzle with the olive oil. Roast for 35-40 mins until soft. Season.

STEP 2

Cook the pasta according to pack instructions. Drain, reserving the water. Use a stick blender to whizz the squash with 400ml cooking water. Heat some oil in a frying pan, fry the sage until crisp, then drain on kitchen paper. Tip the pasta and sauce into the pan and warm through. Scatter with sage.

Barley & broccoli risotto with lemon & basil

Prep: 10 mins **Cook:** 35 mins plus overnight soaking

Serves 2

Ingredients

- 100g wholegrain pearl barley
- 2 tsp reduced-salt vegetable bouillon powder
- 2 tbsp rapeseed oil
- 1 large leek , chopped
- 2 garlic cloves
- ⅔ pack basil
- generous squeeze of lemon juice
- 125g Tenderstem broccoli from a 200g pack

Method

STEP 1

Pour a litre of cold water over the barley, cover and leave to soak overnight.

STEP 2

The next day, drain the barley, reserve the liquid and use it to make 500ml vegetable bouillon. Heat half the oil in a non-stick pan, add the leek and cook briefly to soften. Tip half into a bowl, then add the barley and bouillon to the pan, cover and simmer for 20 mins.

STEP 3

Meanwhile, add the garlic, basil, remaining oil, the lemon juice and 3 tbsp water to the leeks in the bowl, and blitz to a paste with a stick blender

STEP 4

When the barley has cooked for 20 mins, add the broccoli to the pan and cook for 5-10 mins more until both are tender. Stir in the basil purée, heat very briefly (to retain the fragrance), then spoon into bowls to serve.

Melon with mint & feta

Serves 2

Ingredients

- 2 x 5cm wedges of watermelon
- 40g feta , crumbled
- handful chopped mint
- 2 wedges of lime

Method

STEP 1

Take each wedge of melon and slice between the rind and flesh to separate them, then cut downwards to make bite-size chunks. Flick out the seeds, scatter over the feta and mint, and squeeze over the lime before serving.

Chakalaka (Soweto chilli)

Prep:40 mins **Cook:**30 mins

Serves 6 - 8

Ingredients

- 3 tbsp light olive oil , or vegetable oil
- 1 red or white onion , finely chopped
- 6 garlic cloves , crushed
- 1-2 green chillies , deseeded and chopped
- thumb-sized piece ginger , finely grated
- 2 tbsp milk, medium or hot curry powder
- 3 peppers (mix of red, green and yellow), finely chopped
- 5-6 large carrots , grated
- 2 tbsp tomato purée
- 5-6 large tomatoes or 400g can chopped tomatoes
- 2 tsp piri-piri spice blend
- 2 thyme sprigs , leaves only, or 2 tsp dried thyme
- spiced apple chutney , BBQ sauce, jerk sauce or piri-piri sauce to taste (optional)
- 400g can baked beans

To serve

- chopped coriander
- rice or mealie bread (South African cornbread)
- mixed green salad
- grilled meats

Method

STEP 1

Heat the oil in a casserole dish set over a medium heat. Add the onion and cook until soft and starting to caramelise.

STEP 2

Stir in the garlic, chillies and half the ginger. Cook for 1-2 mins, then add the curry powder and stir to make a curry paste. If the mixture is starting to catch, add a splash of water to stop it burning.

STEP 3

Stir in the peppers and cook for 2 mins more. Add the carrots and stir to make sure they are coated in the curry paste. Stir in the purée, tomatoes, piri-piri spice, thyme and apple chutney or sauce, if using.

STEP 4

Add the baked beans, then half-fill the can with water and add that too. Bring to the boil, reduce the heat and simmer for at least 10 mins until the vegetables are tender and the mixture has thickened.

STEP 5

Add the remaining ginger and season to taste. Sprinkle with coriander and serve hot or cold with rice or mealie bread, salad and grilled meats.

Omelette pancakes with tomato & pepper sauce

Prep:10 mins **Cook:**20 mins

Serves 2

Ingredients

- 4 large eggs
- handful basil leaves

For the sauce

- 2 tsp rapeseed oil , plus a little extra for the pancakes
- 1 yellow pepper , quartered, deseeded and thinly sliced
- 2 garlic cloves , thinly sliced
- 1 tbsp cider vinegar
- 400g can chopped tomatoes
- wholemeal bread or salad leaves, to serve

Method

STEP 1

First make the sauce. Heat the oil in a large frying pan, and fry the pepper and garlic for 5 mins to soften them. Spoon in the cider vinegar and allow to sizzle away. Tip in the tomatoes, then measure in a third of a can of water. Cover and leave to simmer for 10-15 mins until the peppers are tender and the sauce is thick.

STEP 2

Meanwhile, make the pancakes. Beat 1 egg with 1 tsp water and seasoning, then heat a small non-stick frying pan with a tiny amount of oil. Add the egg mixture and cook for 1-2 mins until set into a thin pancake. Lift onto a plate, cover with foil and repeat with the other eggs. Roll up onto warm plates, spoon over the sauce and scatter with the basil. Serve with bread or a salad on the side.

Spicy spaghetti with garlic mushrooms

Prep: 10 mins **Cook:** 15 mins

Serves 4

Ingredients

- 2 tbsp olive oil
- 250g pack chestnut mushroom, thickly sliced
- 1 garlic clove, thinly sliced
- small bunch parsley, leaves only
- 1 celery stick, finely chopped
- 1 onion, finely chopped
- 400g can chopped tomato
- 1/2 red chilli, deseeded and finely chopped, (or use drieds chilli flakes)
- 300g spaghetti

Method

STEP 1

Heat 1 tbsp oil in a pan, add the mushrooms, then fry over a high heat for 3 mins until golden and softened. Add the garlic, fry for 1 min more, then tip into a bowl with the parsley. Add the onion and celery to the pan with the rest of the oil, then fry for 5 mins until lightly coloured.

STEP 2

Stir in the tomatoes, chilli and a little salt, then bring to the boil. Reduce the heat and simmer, uncovered, for 10 mins until thickened. Meanwhile, boil the spaghetti, then drain. Toss with the sauce, top with the garlicky mushrooms, then serve.

Teriyaki steak with pak choi & noodles

Prep:10 mins **Cook:**15 mins

Serves 2

Ingredients

- ½ tsp Chinese five-spice powder
- 2 lean beef steak , 175g each
- 1 tbsp sunflower oil
- 2 pak choi , trimmed and quartered
- 1 medium carrot , thinly sliced
- 1 red pepper , deseeded and thinly sliced
- 150g pack straight-to-wok egg noodles
- 3 tbsp teriyaki sauce

Method

STEP 1

Mix the five-spice with 1/2 tsp flaky sea salt and 1/2 tsp black pepper, and rub into the steaks. Heat 1 tsp of the oil in a large, non-stick frying pan over a medium-high heat. Fry the steak for 4-5 mins each side or until done to your liking. Transfer to a warmed plate, cover loosely with foil and leave to rest.

STEP 2

Pour the remaining oil into the pan, add the pak choi, the carrot and pepper. Stir-fry for 3 mins, then add the noodles and stir-fry for 2 mins more.

STEP 3

Pour in the teriyaki sauce and simmer for a few secs, then divide the vegetable noodles between 2 warmed plates or shallow bowls. Slice the steak thickly and place on top.

Speedy Mediterranean gnocchi

Cook:5 mins **Serves 2**

Ingredients

- 400g gnocchi
- 200g chargrilled vegetables (from the deli counter - I used chargrilled peppers, aubergines, artichokes and semi-dried tomatoes)
- 2 tbsp red pesto
- a handful of basil leaves
- parmesan or pecorino (or vegetarian alternative), to serve

Method

STEP 1

Boil a large pan of salted water. Add the gnocchi, cook for 2 mins or until it rises to the surface, then drain and tip back into the pan with a splash of reserved cooking water.

STEP 2

Add the chargrilled veg, chopped into pieces if large, red pesto and basil leaves. Serve with shavings of Parmesan or pecorino (or vegetarian alternative).

Cheat's chicken ramen

Prep:10 mins **Cook:**15 mins - 20 mins

Serves 4

Ingredients

- 1.2l good-quality chicken stock
- small pack coriander, stalks and leaves separated
- 1 red chilli (deseeded if you don't like it too hot), sliced
- 2 tbsp light soy sauce
- 100g grey oyster mushrooms, sliced
- 100g pack baby pak choi
- 2 skinless cooked chicken breasts, sliced

- 100g egg noodles
- 50g sliced bamboo shoots

Method

STEP 1

Set a large saucepan over a medium heat and pour in the stock. Finely chop the coriander stalks and add to the stock with most of the chilli. Bring to the boil and add 200ml water. Once boiled, reduce the heat and simmer for 5-10 mins to infuse the coriander and chilli.

STEP 2

Add the soy sauce and a grinding of black pepper, then the mushrooms, pak choi, chicken and noodles. Simmer for 2 mins until the noodles soften, before adding the bamboo shoots.

STEP 3

Serve in deep bowls topped with coriander leaves and the remaining chilli slices.

Mushroom jacket potatoes

Prep: 10 mins **Cook:** 1 hr and 25 mins

Serves 2

Ingredients

- 2 large potatoes
- 2 tsp sunflower oil
- 250g mushrooms
- 100g sour cream & chive dip
- sprigs of dill (to garnish)

Method

STEP 1

Heat oven to 200C/180C fan/gas 6. Prick the potatoes all over with a fork and rub with half the sunflower oil. Bake the potatoes for 1 hr 20 mins.

STEP 2

Slice the mushrooms, fry in the remaining oil, then stir through half the sour cream & chive dip. Pile the mushrooms into the jacket potatoes and garnish with dill.

Dhal with garam masala carrots

Prep:5 mins **Cook:**20 mins

Serves 1

Ingredients

- 75g red lentils
- 1 garlic clove , peeled
- knob of salted butter
- 2 carrots , cut into batons
- 1 tbsp rapeseed oil
- ½ tsp garam masala
- 1 tsp nigella seeds (kalonji, optional)
- 1 tsp Greek yogurt

Method

STEP 1

Cook the lentils in 500ml water with the garlic clove for around 20 mins until the lentils are tender. Fish the garlic clove out, crush it and stir it back into the lentils with the butter. Season well. It should be spoonable like a thick soup – keep simmering if it's not thick enough.

STEP 2

Put the carrots in a pan, just cover with water, bring to the boil and simmer until just tender, about 8-10 mins. Drain, then toss in the oil and garam masala. Tip into a frying pan and fry until the carrots start to brown, then add the nigella seeds, if using, and fry for another min.

STEP 3

Serve the dhal in a bowl with the yogurt and carrots, with the remaining spices and oil from the pan on top.

Spicy turkey sweet potatoes

Prep:5 mins **Cook:**45 mins

Serves 4

Ingredients

- 4 sweet potatoes
- 1 tbsp olive oil
- 1 onion , finely chopped
- 1 garlic clove , crushed
- 500g pack turkey thigh mince
- 500g carton passata
- 3 tbsp barbecue sauce
- ½ tsp cayenne pepper
- 4 tbsp soured cream
- ½ pack chives , finely snipped

Method

STEP 1

Heat oven to 200C/180C fan/gas 6. Prick the potatoes, place on a baking tray and bake for 45 mins or until really soft.

STEP 2

Meanwhile, heat the oil in a frying pan, add the onion and cook gently for 8 mins until softened. Stir in the garlic, then tip in the mince and stir to break up. Cook over a high heat until any liquid has evaporated and the mince is browned, about 10 mins. Pour in the passata, then fill the carton a quarter full of water and tip that in too. Add the barbecue sauce and cayenne, then lower the heat and simmer gently for 15 mins, adding a little extra water if needed. Taste and season.

STEP 3

When the potatoes are soft, split them down the centre and spoon the mince over the top. Add a dollop of soured cream and a sprinkling of chives.

Singapore chilli crab

Prep:25 mins **Cook:**5 mins

Serves 2

Ingredients

- 1 whole cooked crab (about 1kg)
- 2 tbsp flavourless oil
- 3 garlic cloves , very finely chopped
- thumb-sized piece ginger , very finely chopped
- 3 red chillies , 2 very finely chopped, 1 sliced
- 4 tbsp tomato ketchup
- 2 tbsp soy sauce
- handful coriander leaves, roughly chopped
- 2 spring onions , sliced
- rice or steamed bad buns, to serve

Method

STEP 1

The crab must be prepared before stir-frying (you can ask your fishmonger to do this). This involves removing the claws, the main shell, discarding the dead man's fingers, then cutting the body into four pieces, and cracking the claws and the legs so the sauce can get through to the meat.

STEP 2

Heat the oil in a large wok and sizzle the garlic, ginger and chopped chillies for 1 min or until fragrant. Add the ketchup, soy and 100ml water, and stir to combine. Throw in the crab, turn up the heat and stir-fry for 3-5 mins or until the crab is piping hot and coated in the sauce. Stir through most of the coriander, spring onions and sliced chilli.

STEP 3

Use tongs to arrange the crab on a serving dish, pour over the sauce from the pan and scatter over the remaining coriander, spring onions and sliced chilli. Serve with rice or bao buns, and a lot of napkins.

Baked falafel & cauliflower tabbouleh

Prep:30 mins **Cook:**20 mins

Serves 6

Ingredients

- 3 x 400g cans chickpeas , drained (or 250g dried chickpeas, soaked in 1 litre cold water overnight, then drained)
- 3 tsp ground cumin
- 2 tsp ground coriander
- 1 tsp cayenne pepper
- 1 red onion , quartered
- 3 garlic cloves
- 2 tbsp sesame seeds
- 1 ½ tsp baking powder (gluten-free, if you like)
- 2 small packs parsley , stalks and leaves separated, leaves chopped
- 4 tbsp olive oil
- 1 cauliflower , cut into large florets
- 1 small pack mint , leaves chopped and stalks discarded
- 1 lemon , juiced

Method

STEP 1

Heat oven to 200C/180C fan/gas 6 and line two baking sheets with baking parchment. Tip the chickpeas, 2 tsp of the ground cumin, 1 tsp of the ground coriander, the cayenne pepper, onion, garlic, sesame seeds, baking powder, parsley stalks and 1 tbsp water into a food processor. Blitz until combined but not smooth (you want the falafel to have some texture, rather than being the consistency of hummus). Season to taste, then roll into 18 evenly sized balls. Flatten each ball into a disc shape and arrange on the baking sheets, then brush the tops with 1 tbsp of the oil. Bake for 20 mins until golden and crisp, turning halfway through cooking.

STEP 2

Meanwhile, clean out the food processor, then tip in the cauliflower and briefly pulse until it resembles couscous. Mix the cauliflower couscous with the remaining ground spices and olive oil, then add some seasoning. Tip onto a roasting tray and roast for 10-12 mins until lightly toasted, stirring occasionally.

STEP 3

Remove from the oven and leave to cool, then mix through the parsley leaves, mint leaves and lemon juice. Season to taste. Will keep for three days in the fridge. Serve the baked falafel with the cauliflower tabbouleh and some salad, if you like.

Lentil fritters

Prep: 15 mins **Cook:** 10 mins

Serves 2

Ingredients

- 300g leftover basic lentils
- handful of chopped coriander
- 1 chopped spring onion
- 50g gram flour
- 2 carrots
- 2 courgettes
- ½ tsp sesame seeds
- handful of coriander
- ½ tsp sesame oil
- juice of 1 lime
- 1 tbsp rapeseed oil

Method

STEP 1

Mix the leftover lentils with the chopped coriander, spring onion and gram flour, then set aside. Use a peeler to cut the carrots and courgettes into long ribbons, then toss the ribbons with the sesame seeds and coriander in sesame oil and the lime juice.

STEP 2

Heat the rapeseed oil in a frying pan. Spoon in four dollops of the lentil mixture and flatten into patties. Fry each side until golden and serve with the ribbon salad.

Layered aubergine & lentil bake

Prep: 15 mins **Cook:** 45 mins

Serves 4

Ingredients

- 2 aubergines , cut into 0.5cm slices lengthways
- 3 tbsp olive oil
- 140g puy lentils
- 2 onions , finely chopped
- 3 garlic cloves , finely chopped
- 300g cooked butternut squash
- 400g can chopped tomato
- ½ small pack basil leaves
- 125g ball of mozzarella , torn

Method

STEP 1

Heat oven to 220C/200C fan/gas 7. Brush both sides of the aubergine slices with 2 tbsp of the oil, lay on baking sheets, season and bake for 15-20 mins until tender, turning once. Cook the lentils following pack instructions.

STEP 2

Heat the remaining oil in a large frying pan. Tip in the onions and garlic and cook until soft. Stir though the squash and the tomatoes, plus ½ can of water. Simmer for 10-15 mins until the sauce has thickened. Stir in the lentils, basil and seasoning.

STEP 3

Spoon a layer of lentils into a small baking dish. Top with aubergine slices and repeat, finishing with a layer of aubergine. Scatter with mozzarella and bake for a further 15 mins until the cheese is golden and bubbling.

Stir-fried pork with ginger & honey

Prep:15 mins **Cook:**10 mins

Serves 2

Ingredients

- 2 nests medium egg noodles
- 2 tsp cornflour
- 2 tbsp soy sauce
- 1 tbsp honey
- 1 tbsp sunflower oil
- 250g/9oz pork tenderloin, cut into bite-sized pieces
- thumb-sized piece ginger, finely chopped
- 2 garlic cloves, finely chopped
- 1 green pepper, deseeded and sliced
- 100g mange tout
- 1 tsp sesame seed

Method

STEP 1

Bring a pan of salted water to the boil and cook the noodles following pack instructions. Meanwhile, mix the cornflour with 1 tbsp water, then stir in the soy sauce and honey, and set aside.

STEP 2

Heat the oil in a wok over a high heat. Add the pork and cook for 2 mins until browned all over. Add the ginger, garlic, pepper and mangetout, and cook for a further 2 mins. Reduce the heat, then add the soy and honey mixture, stirring and cooking until the sauce bubbles and thickens. Divide the drained noodles between 2 bowls. Top with the pork and vegetables, and finish with a sprinkling of sesame seeds.

Easy pulled beef ragu

Prep:20 mins **Cook:**4 hrs

8 (or 2 meals for 4)

Ingredients

- 2 tbsp olive oil
- 1kg boneless beef brisket
- 2 onions , finely chopped
- 4 garlic cloves , finely chopped

- 5 carrots , thickly sliced
- 250ml red wine
- 2 x 400g cans chopped tomatoes
- 2 tbsp tomato purée
- 4 bay leaves
- 450g large pasta shapes (such as paccheri, rigate or rigatoni)
- large handful basil leaves , to serve
- grated parmesan , to serve

Method

STEP 1

Heat oven to 150C/130C fan/gas 2. Heat 1 tbsp oil in a flameproof casserole dish and brown the beef all over. Take the beef out of the dish, add the remaining oil and gently cook the onions and garlic for 10 mins until softened.

STEP 2

Add the browned beef back to the dish with the carrots, red wine, tomatoes, tomato purée and bay leaves. Cover with foil and a lid, and slowly cook for 3 - 3 1/2 hrs or until the meat falls apart. Check on it a couple of times, turning the beef over and giving it a good stir to make sure it's coated in the sauce.

STEP 3

Cook the pasta following pack instructions, then drain. Shred the beef – it should just fall apart when you touch it with a fork – then spoon the beef and tomato sauce over the pasta. Scatter with basil and Parmesan before serving.

Almond crêpes with avocado & nectarines

Prep:10 mins **Cook:**5 mins

Serves 2

Ingredients

- 2 large eggs
- 3 tbsp ground almonds
- 2 tsp rapeseed oil

- 1 avocado , halved, stoned and flesh lightly crushed
- 2 ripe nectarines , stoned and sliced
- seeds from 1/2 pomegranate
- ½ lime , cut into 2 wedges, for squeezing over

Method

STEP 1

Beat one egg and 1 1 /2 tbsp of the almonds in a small bowl with 1 tbsp water. Heat 1 tsp oil in a large non-stick frying pan over a medium heat and pour in the egg mixture, swirling the pan to evenly cover the base. Cook until the mixture sets and turns golden on the underside, about 2 mins. (There is no need to flip it over.) Turn it out onto a plate and make another one with 1 tbsp water, the remaining egg, oil and almonds.

STEP 2

Top each crêpe with the avocado, nectarines and pomegranate, and squeeze over the lime at the table.

Skinny lamb biryani

Prep:15 mins **Cook:**20 mins

Serves 2

Ingredients

For the cauliflower pilau

- 350g cauliflower florets
- ½ tsp turmeric
- 3 cardamom pods , lightly crushed
- ½ tsp fennel seeds , lightly crushed
- a few pinches of black onion seeds or nigella seeds

For the spicy lamb

- 1 tbsp rapeseed oil
- 1 large onion , finely chopped
- 1 tbsp finely chopped ginger

- 1 red chilli , deseeded and finely chopped
- 2 garlic cloves , thinly sliced
- 1 tsp ground cumin
- 1 tsp ground coriander
- 200g very lean lamb steak, cut into bite-sized pieces
- 200g can chopped tomatoes
- 1 tsp bouillon
- 15g toasted flaked almonds
- 50g pomegranate seeds
- handful small mint leaves

Method

STEP 1

Put the cauliflower in a food processor and pulse until it is reduced to rice-sized pieces. Tip into a large bowl and stir in the turmeric, cardamom, fennel seeds, black onion seeds and some seasoning. Cover with cling film, pierce and set aside.

STEP 2

For the spicy lamb, heat the oil in a non-stick wok and fry the onion and ginger for 10 mins until soft and golden. Add the chilli and garlic, and cook for 1 min more.

STEP 3

Stir in the cumin and coriander, cook briefly, then toss in the lamb and stir-fry for 1-2 mins until pale brown. Add the tomatoes and the bouillon, and cook for 2 mins - you are aiming for a thick sauce and really tender lamb that is still a little pink and juicy.

STEP 4

Meanwhile, put the cauliflower in the microwave and cook on high for 3 mins. Tip out onto serving plates, dot the lamb and sauce in patches over the rice, then scatter with the almonds, pomegranate seeds and mint leaves to serve.

Lighter spaghetti & meatballs

Prep:30 mins **Cook:**35 mins

Serves 4

Ingredients

- 1 tsp rapeseed oil
- 280g spaghetti

For the meatballs

- 200g green lentils (well drained weight from a 400g can)
- 250g lean minced pork (max 8% fat)
- ½ tsp finely chopped rosemary
- ½ tsp Dijon mustard
- 1 garlic clove , crushed

For the sauce

- 1 tbsp rapeseed oil
- 2 shallots , finely chopped
- 2 garlic cloves , finely chopped
- 500g cherry tomatoes , preferably on the vine, halved
- 2 tsp tomato purée
- pinch of chilli flakes
- 2 tbsp chopped oregano , plus a few chopped leaves to garnish

Method

STEP 1

Heat oven to 200C/180C fan/gas 6. Line a baking sheet with foil and brush with 1 tsp oil. Mash the lentils in a bowl with the back of a fork to break down a bit, but not completely. Stir in the pork, rosemary, mustard, garlic, some pepper to generously season, and mix well with the fork to distribute the lentils evenly. Divide the mixture into 4. Form each quarter into 5 small balls – to give you 20 in total – squeezing the mixture together well as you shape it. Lay the meatballs on the foil and roll them around in the oil to coat all over. Bake for 15 mins until cooked and lightly browned. Remove (leave the oven on) and set aside.

STEP 2

While the meatballs cook, heat 2 tsp of the oil for the sauce in a large non-stick frying pan. Tip in the shallots and garlic, and fry on a medium heat for 3-4 mins until softened and tinged brown. Pour in the remaining 1 tsp oil, lay the tomatoes in the pan so most of them are cut-side down (to help release the juices), raise the heat and fry them for 3-4 mins or until the tomatoes are starting to soften and release their juices. Don't stir, or they may lose their shape. Splash in 125-150ml water so it all bubbles, and gently mix in the tomato purée. Lower the heat and simmer for 2 mins to create a juicy, chunky sauce. Season with the chilli flakes, oregano, pepper and a pinch of salt, and give it a quick stir, adding a drop more water if needed – you want it thick enough to coat the meatballs.

STEP 3

Pour the sauce into a casserole dish, add the meatballs and spoon the sauce over them to coat. Cover with foil and bake for 10 mins while you cook the spaghetti.

STEP 4

Boil a large saucepan of water. Add the spaghetti, stir and bring back to the boil. Cook for 10-12 mins, or following pack instructions, until al dente. Drain well, season with pepper and serve with the meatballs, sauce and a light sprinkling of oregano.

Chocolate-orange steamed pudding with chocolate sauce

Prep:25 mins **Cook:**1 hr and 30 mins

Serves 8

Ingredients

For the chocolate sauce

- 50g cocoa
- 50g butter , plus extra for greasing
- 100g Total Sweet (xylitol, see tip)
- 1 tsp vanilla extract
- 200ml semi-skimmed milk

For the pudding

- 1 small orange
- 100g Total Sweet (xylitol)
- 225g self-raising flour

- 50g cocoa
- 150ml semi-skimmed milk
- 1 tsp vanilla extract
- 2 large eggs

Method

STEP 1

First, make the sauce. Sift the cocoa into a small saucepan, add all the other ingredients, then warm over a medium-high heat, stirring. Allow to bubble hard for 1 min to make a glossy sauce. Spoon 4 tbsp into the base of a lightly buttered, traditional 1.2 litre pudding basin. Leave the rest to cool, stirring occasionally.

STEP 2

Put a very large pan (deep enough to enclose the whole pudding basin) of water on to boil with a small upturned plate placed in the base of the pan to support the basin.

STEP 3

Zest the orange, then cut the peel and pith away, and cut between the membrane to release the segments. Put all the pudding ingredients, except the orange segments, in a food processor and blitz until smooth. Add the orange segments and pulse to chop them into the pudding mixture. Spoon the mixture into the pudding basin, smoothing to the edges.

STEP 4

Tear off a sheet of foil and a sheet of baking parchment, both about 30cm long. Butter the baking parchment and use to cover the foil. Fold a 3cm pleat in the middle of the sheets, then place over the pudding, buttered baking parchment-side down. Tie with string under the lip of the basin, making a handle as you go. Trim the excess parchment and foil to about 5cm, then tuck the foil around the parchment to seal. Lower the basin into the pan of water, checking that the water comes tw o-thirds of the way up the sides of the basin, then cover the pan with a lid to trap the steam and simmer for 1 1/2 hours.

STEP 5

Carefully unwrap the pudding – it should now be risen and firm – and turn out of the basin on to a plate. Spoon over some warmed sauce and serve the rest separately with slices of the pudding.

Bean & barley soup

Prep: 5 mins **Cook:** 1 hr

Serves 4

Ingredients

- 2 tbsp vegetable oil
- 1 large onion , finely chopped
- 1 fennel bulb , quartered, cored and sliced
- 5 garlic cloves , crushed
- 400g can chickpea , drained and rinsed
- 2 x 400g cans chopped tomatoes
- 600ml vegetable stock
- 250g pearl barley
- 215g can butter beans , drained and rinsed
- 100g pack baby spinach leaves
- grated parmesan , to serve

Method

STEP 1

Heat the oil in a saucepan over a medium heat, add the onion, fennel and garlic, and cook until softened and just beginning to brown, about 10-12 mins.

STEP 2

Mash half the chickpeas and add to the pan with the tomatoes, stock and barley. Top up with a can of water and bring to the boil, then reduce the heat and simmer, covered, for 45 mins or until the barley is tender. Add another can of water if the liquid has significantly reduced.

STEP 3

Add the remaining chickpeas and the butter beans to the soup. After a few mins, stir in the spinach and cook until wilted, about 1 min. Season and serve scattered with Parmesan.

Cloud bread

Prep:10 mins **Cook:**20 mins

makes 8 pieces

Ingredients

- oil or butter for greasing
- 4 eggs, separated
- 50g cream cheese
- ¼ tsp cream of tartar
- ½ tsp nigella seeds

Method

STEP 1

Heat oven to 150C/130C fan/gas 2 and line 2 large baking sheets with baking paper, then grease well with butter or oil.

STEP 2

In a large bowl and using electric beaters, whisk the egg whites together until stiff peaks form. You should be able to carefully turn the bowl upside down without it falling out.

STEP 3

In another bowl, put the egg yolks, cream cheese and cream of tartar then whisk together (no need to wash the beaters first) until smooth, pale and frothy. Next, fold the egg whites, a spoonful at a time into the yolk mixture, be as gentle as you can with this so you don't knock out too much of the air and finally fold in the nigella seeds and season with salt and pepper.

STEP 4

Carefully dollop the mixture onto the prepared baking sheets, if the mixture is a little runny when you get to the bottom of the bowl don't use the last few spoonfuls – only use the really fluffy mix on the top. Bake for 20 mins or until lightly golden and craggy on top. Allow to cool for a few moments before carefully removing from the paper with a palette knife.

Creamy tomato soup

Prep:30 mins **Cook:**45 mins

Serves 6 adults and 6 kids

Ingredients

- 3 tbsp olive oil
- 2 onions, chopped
- 2 celery sticks, chopped
- 300g carrot, chopped
- 500g potato, diced
- 4 bay leaves
- 5 tbsp tomato purée
- 2 tbsp sugar
- 2 tbsp red or white wine vinegar
- 4 x 400g cans chopped tomatoes
- 500g passata
- 3 vegetable stock cubes
- 400ml whole milk

Method

STEP 1

Put the oil, onions, celery, carrots, potatoes and bay leaves in a big casserole dish, or two saucepans. Fry gently until the onions are softened – about 10-15 mins. Fill the kettle and boil it.

STEP 2

Stir in the tomato purée, sugar, vinegar, chopped tomatoes and passata, then crumble in the stock cubes. Add 1 litre boiling water and bring to a simmer. Cover and simmer for 15 mins until the potato is tender, then remove the bay leaves. Purée with a stick blender (or ladle into a blender in batches) until very smooth. Season to taste and add a pinch more sugar if it needs it. The soup can now be cooled and chilled for up to 2 days, or frozen for up to 3 months.

STEP 3

To serve, reheat the soup, stirring in the milk – try not to let it boil. Serve in small bowls for the children with cheesy sausage rolls then later in bowls for the adults as Hot Bloody Mary soup (see 'Goes well with' recipes, below).

Manufactured by Amazon.ca
Acheson, AB